Alto's

Creative Mat Designs

Design Collection 1

Publisher: Alto's EZ Mat, Inc.
            703 North Wenas St.
            Ellensburg, WA 98926-2861

Toll Free: 800-225-2497
Phone: 509-962-9212
Fax: 509-962-3127
email: altosmat@eburg.com
internet: www.altosezmat.com

© Alto's EZ Mat, Inc. 1997
ISBN 0-9658215-0-1
Printed in the U.S.A.

Reprints of the first thirteen CUT-by-CUT designs from #1 to #0306.

Introduction

Welcome.

Within this volume you will find step-by-step instructions showing the intricacies of Creative Mat Designs.

Presentation is important in many walks of life, none more so than the world of art. Any piece of work is incomplete until it is ready for display. We at Alto's believe that the matting of artwork is more than simply decoration, but an integral part of the work being framed.

This book shows designs of varying styles and complexity, each appropriate for different types of artwork. It is our hope, however, that these designs will serve not as an end, but as a beginning. Once you have gained success and confidence with the designs in this book, you will be able to expand upon the techniques and create your own mat designs.

Above all, we hope you will enjoy the creative process while making beautiful and artistic mats for your own art treasures.

Basics review and a few notes

A well cut mat has the following:
- Cleanly cut corners, with no curves, tears or obvious overcuts.
- Smooth inner edges, with a straight 45° bevel along the entire length of the cut.
- Edges of multiple layered mats that are perfectly parallel.
- Mat surfaces that are clean, with no pencil or other marks.
- Mat colors that are suitable for the artwork.
- The shape of the design, border widths, and line widths are proportioned for good balance, and the mat has been cut to fit the artwork and the frame.

It is important to be familiar with Alto's Mat Cutting Systems to master the designs of this book.

Remember – before you start cutting, the pencil lines you draw are always used to start and stop your cuts — don't use the actual cuts as your reference. (This is true for most of the mats you will cut with your Alto's Mat Cutting System.) Start your cut by pivoting the blade into the matboard on the "start" pencil line, and pick the blade back up on the "stop" pencil line. Otherwise two things can happen: 1) If you overcut the lines, you may cut through the sides of the main window and lose the corner design element of that particular mat, or 2) If you undercut lines, pieces won't fall out and you will have to recut.

Tools and materials needed to cut all thirteen of these mats:
Alto's 4501 or 4505 Mat Cutting System, Alto's Oval Template Set, Alto's Model 360 Circle Cutter, Various Colors of Matboard, Blades, Double-Stick Tape, Glue, Soft Eraser, Ruler, 30-60-90 Triangle, and a Sharp Pencil.

Table of Contents

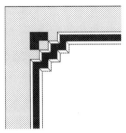

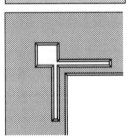

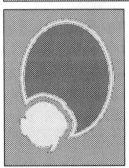
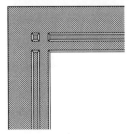
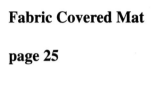

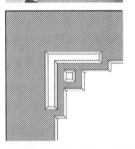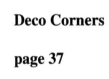

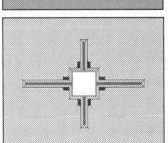

Stepped Mosaics

*A*lthough there are many steps involved, this double mat with stepped mosaic corners will be simple to cut if you read and follow these instructions. You should be familiar with mosaic tiles and corners (see 4501/4505 instructions, p. 16).

This mat uses <u>two different colors</u> of matboard. Both the top and bottom mat should be cut from matboard that is the <u>same thickness</u>. The outside dimensions of the bottom piece of matboard will be slightly smaller than the outside dimensions of the top piece. Learn this pattern on practice matboard first.

Materials: Alto's 4501 or 4505 Mat Cutting System. You will also need two pieces of matboard, 11" x 14" and 10-1/2" x 13-1/2", double-stick tape, a new blade, glue, and a sharp pencil.

1 **Place an 11" x 14" piece of matboard under the straight-edge and set the dimensioning system at 2".** Draw reference lines for each of the four sides of the window opening. Draw lines <u>out to the edges</u> of the matboard (**Diagram A**).

2 **Cut all four sides of the window opening.** The window scrap piece should fall out leaving you with a single mat. This is the top mat. Set it aside and keep the window scrap piece (**no diagram**).

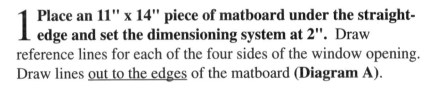

Reference lines drawn with the Dimensioning System set at 2"

A 2" 2" 2"

3 **Cut a second piece of matboard a little smaller than the top mat (approximately 10-1/2" x 13-1/2").** This is the bottom mat. Replace the window scrap piece in the top mat. Attach the smaller mat, face down to the back of the top mat with double-stick tape (**Diagram B**). Make sure to use only a small amount of tape on the window scrap piece so that you will be able to separate the two pieces later. The window scrap pieces will be used to cut the mosaic tiles.

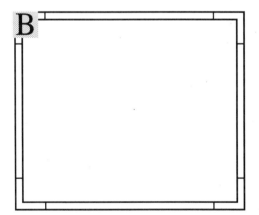

B

4 **Place the two attached pieces of matboard under the straightedge and set the dimensioning system at 2-1/4".** Draw main outside reference lines for all four sides of the window opening (**Diagram C**).

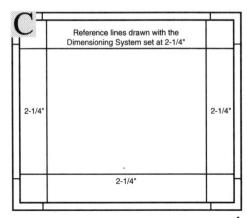

C Reference lines drawn with the Dimensioning System set at 2-1/4"

2-1/4" 2-1/4" 2-1/4"

Focus on EACH cut to see: – where is the START – where is the STOP – <u>then</u>, and only then, cut.

5 Draw intersecting start/stop reference lines by moving the cutting guide in 1/4" steps. Look at **Diagram D** and do this on all four sides. The dimensioning system settings are 2-1/2", 2-3/4", and 3".

D

Dimensioning System settings

2-1/2"
2-3/4"
3"

6 Erase the extra lines so that your reference lines look like **Diagram E.** This is very important. The reference lines for the stepped corners will not be confusing if you follow this instruction.

E

OUTSIDE CORNER CUT SAMPLE
To cut this type of corner the cuts need to cross correctly. Look at **Diagram F** and notice how <u>the cuts cross on an outside corner</u>.

F

Cut

Cut

7 Look at **Diagram G.** For the <u>bottom</u> left corner cut start at the appropriate start reference line and cut into the window scrap. For the <u>top</u> left corner cut, start in the window scrap and stop on the appropriate stop reference line. Using the start and stop reference lines, move the cutting guide in 1/4" increments and cut the small stepped corners in all four corners of the mat. Cut the final long cuts with the dimensioning system set at 2-1/4" and the whole window scrap piece should come free.

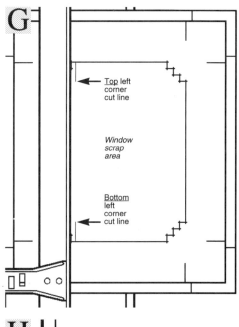

G

<u>Top</u> left corner cut line

Window scrap area

<u>Bottom</u> left corner cut line

Diagram H shows what one of your four corners will look like after all of the cuts have been made.

H

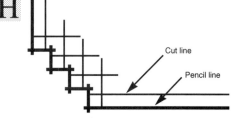

Cut line

Pencil line

Design: Stepped Mosaics

DRAW REFERENCE LINES FOR THE "L" SHAPED MOSAIC TILES. Separate the two window scrap pieces from each other and clean off the double-stick tape by rubbing it with the pad of your thumb. **It is important <u>not to let the window scrap piece move</u> when you are marking and cutting the matboard in the following steps.** If the matboard moves at any time, the "L" shaped mosaic tiles won't fit.

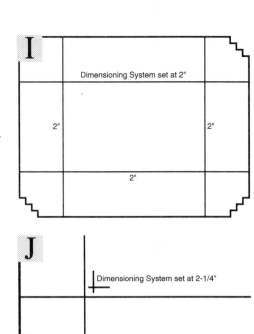

I

Dimensioning System set at 2"

2" 2"

2"

8 Place the window scrap piece from the bottom mat (or a piece of the same color) under the straightedge and set the dimensioning system at 2". Draw reference lines as you would for a single mat (**Diagram I**).

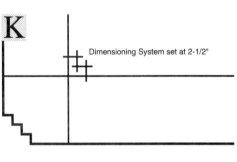

J

Dimensioning System set at 2-1/4"

9 Set the dimensioning system at 2-1/4". Draw reference lines approximately 1" long at each of the four corners as illustrated (**Diagram J**).

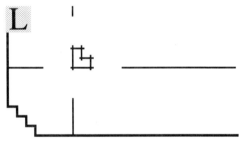

K

Dimensioning System set at 2-1/2"

10 Set the dimensioning system at 2-1/2". Draw reference lines approximately 1" long at each of the four corners as illustrated (**Diagram K**).

L

11 Erase the extra lines so that your reference lines look like Diagram L. This is very important. The reference lines for the "L" shaped mosaic tiles will not be confusing if you follow this instruction.

CUT THE "L" SHAPED MOSAIC TILES. Only the inner corner cut start and stop reference points are crucial. All other cuts need to cross.

12 Set the dimensioning system at 2-1/2". Cut the eight lines.

13 Set the dimensioning system at 2-1/4". Cut the eight lines.

14 Set the dimensioning system at 2". Cut the eight lines. Slide the "L" shaped mosaic tiles out (see **Diagram M**). Set the "L" shaped mosaic tiles aside. Before you go to the next step, check to make sure the "L" shaped mosaic tiles fit in the corner of the top single mat. If they don't fit, the window scrap piece moved when you made your cuts; you will have to repeat Steps 8 through 14 using a piece of the same colored matboard.

M

CUT 1/4" MOSAIC TILES (see 4501/4505 instructions, p. 16). 1/4" mosaic tiles are hard to work with, so we will cut more than we actually use. Be sure to hold the matboard down firmly and tight against the stops each time you move the dimensioning system. Also be sure to keep the cutter tight against the straightedge as you make each cut.

15 **Place the window scrap piece from the top mat under the straightedge and set the dimensioning system at 2".** Make a cut in the middle of the piece of matboard (**Diagram N**). Do <u>not</u> cut edge to edge.

N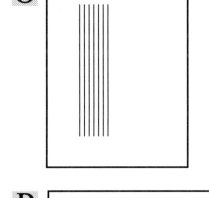

16 **Set the dimensioning system at 2-1/4".** Make cuts as in Step 15, moving the dimensioning system 1/4" before you make each cut, until you have a total of seven cuts (**Diagram O**). Measurements are: 2-1/4", 2-1/2", 2-3/4", 3", 3-1/4", 3-1/2", 3-3/4".

17 **Turn the window piece 90°, place it under the straightedge and set the dimensioning system at 2-1/2".** Make cuts as in Step 16, moving the dimensioning system 1/4" before you make each cut, until you have a total of seven cuts (**Diagram P**). The 1/4" mosaic tiles should fall out.

GLUE THE MOSAIC TILES TO THE DOUBLE MAT.
Make sure your hands are clean. Use only a tiny bit of white glue for each mosaic tile or it will ooze out and stain the matboard.

18 **First glue the four "L" shaped mosaic tiles into the corners of the window opening.** You may have to move the tiles to adjust them so that they fit perfectly into each corner (**Diagram Q**).

19 **Find twelve 1/4" mosaic tiles (three for each corner) that fit perfectly (not all tiles will).** Glue them to the mat next to the "L" shaped mosaic tiles (**Diagram R**). The "L" shaped mosaic tiles will now have the appearance of being inlaid.

Now that you understand how to cut this mat, you can change the dimensions of the window openings to fit the particular dimensions of whatever you are matting.

Have fun!

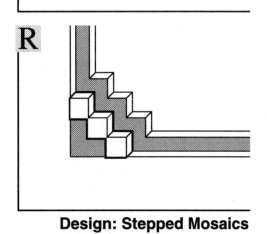

4

Design: Stepped Mosaics

Title Block

This double mat is done in four stages. First, draw all lines on the back of the mat and label the far cut*. Second, cut the far cut and the regular cuts. Third, attach a second piece of smaller matboard to the back of the first. Fourth and last, repeat the whole process with a 1/4" difference in measurements for the liner.

Materials: Alto's 4501 or 4505 Mat Cutting System. You will also need a piece of 11" x 14" matboard, a piece of 10-1/2" x 13-1/2" matboard, double-stick tape, a fresh cutting blade, and for accuracy, use a very sharp pencil and draw all lines with sharpened tip directly against the straightedge.

1 **Start with an 11" x 14" piece of matboard and set the dimensioning system at 2".** Draw reference lines "a", "b", and "c" for the top and both sides of the window opening. Draw lines all the way out to the edges as shown. Draw line "d", the bottom of your title bar opening **(Diagram A)**.

2 **Set the dimensioning system at 4".** Draw the bottom line of the window opening ("h") all the way to the mat's edges as shown **(Diagram A)**.

3 **Set the dimensioning system at 3-1/2".** Draw the top of the title bar and its two short sides, lines "e", "f", and "g" **(Diagram A)**. Make small reference marks <u>at the edge of the matboard</u> for all four of the lines that make the title bar, "d", "e", "f", and "g" **(Diagram A)**.

4 <u>Label</u> the far cut as shown **(Diagram B)**. It is the top line of the title bar.

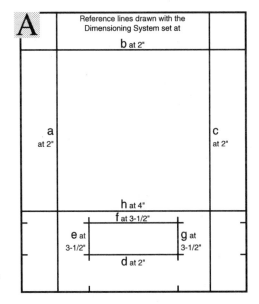

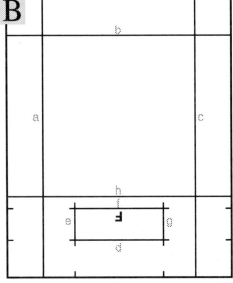

*Far cuts are cuts made farther, or beyond, the standard reach[1] of the dimensioning system. How this is done is explained in Step 5. For many of you this concept will not become clear until you actually do it. For this Title Block mat, there is <u>one</u> far cut on the top mat and one on the bottom mat.

[1] The standard reach of the 4501 dimensioning system is 6". The 4505 dimension system will reach out to 8".

5 **Cut the far cut.** First, set the dimensioning system at 5". Next, slide the mat under the straightedge as shown **(Diagram C)**. Stop as soon as the straightedge lines up with the "F" labeled far cut line. When it is perfectly lined up, cut.

6 **Set the dimensioning system back at 3-1/2".** Cut the two short sides of the rectangular title bar, lines "e" and "g" **(no diagram)**.

7 **Now set it back at 2".** First cut the bottom of the title bar, line "d", then cut the top three sides of the window opening, lines "a", "b", and "c" **(Diagram A)**.

8 **Set the dimensioning system at 4".** Make the last cut—the bottom line of the window opening, line "h" **(no diagram)**. The two window pieces should fall out, leaving you with a single mat with a rectangular title bar. Keep these two window pieces (from the main opening and the title bar).

9 **DOUBLE MAT (see 4501/4505 instructions, p. 10).** Replace the window pieces on the top mat. Attach the smaller 10-1/2" x 13-1/2" mat, face down to the back of the first mat with double-stick tape. Put a little tape on the two window pieces to adhere them to the second mat **(Diagram D)**. Center the tape in the title bar window to prevent the sides from sticking.

10 **Repeat Steps 1-4 on the bottom mat except with a 1/4" difference in measurements for a 1/4" liner.**
Repeat Step 1, but with the dimensioning system set at 2-1/4". Repeat Step 2, but with the dimensioning system set at 4-1/4". Repeat Step 3, but with the dimensioning system set at 3-3/4" for the short sides of the title bar. For the top of the title bar, set at 3-1/4". This line is the only far cut—so label it "F" **(Diagram E)**.

11 **Using these new measurements, repeat Steps 5-8 in the same order as before.** First cut the far cut, then the rest of the title bar cuts, and finally the main window opening cuts. When the last cut is made, the window pieces will fall out, leaving you with a beautiful double mat with title bar.

Now that you understand how to cut this mat, you may change the dimensions of both the window opening and the title bar to fit the particular dimensions of whatever you are matting. When using your own dimensions, you will need the reference marks in Step 3.

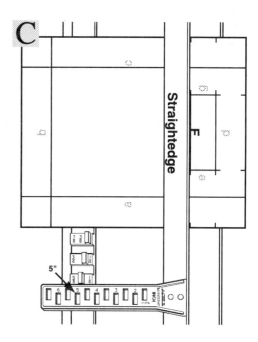

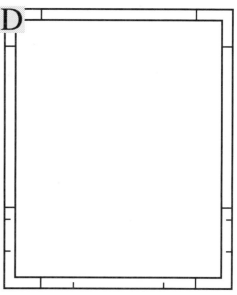

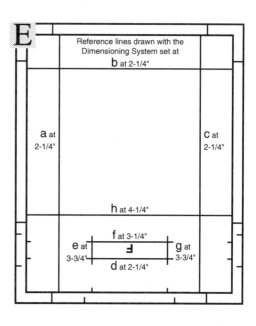

Design: Title Block

Extended Corners

Focus on EACH cut to see: – where is the START – where is the STOP – then, and only then, cut.

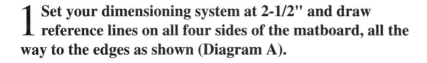

W e'll make this mat in three stages: first, we'll draw all reference lines for all cuts and label our far cuts*, second, we'll cut the far cuts, third, we'll cut the regular cuts. Sounds simple? Well it <u>is</u>, and here are specific step-by-step instructions. **All of the drawing and cutting of this mat takes place on the back of the matboard.** Learn this pattern on a practice matboard first.

    Materials: Alto's 4501 or 4505 Mat Cutting System. *For the 4505 add 1/8" to all measurements on this design.* You will also need a piece of 11" x 14" matboard, clean hands, a fresh cutting blade, and for accuracy, use a very sharp pencil and draw all lines with sharpened tip directly against the straightedge.

1 Set your dimensioning system at 2-1/2" and draw reference lines on all four sides of the matboard, all the way to the edges as shown (Diagram A).

2 Move the dimensioning system to 1-1/2". Draw the 1" squares at the mat's corners, this will mean drawing eight short lines, two on each of the four sides of the mat (**Diagram A**).

3 Set the dimensioning system at 5". Draw the ends of the eight rectangles as shown (**Diagram A**).

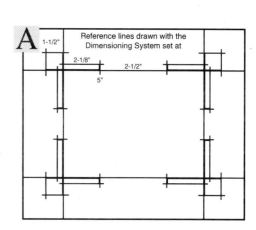

4 Now, set the dimensioning system at 2-1/8". Draw the 3/8" wide rectangles attached to the corner squares. Again, this will be eight lines, two on each mat side (**Diagram A**).

5 Label all of your far cuts with the letter "F" The window line is being used for two cuts (**Diagram B**). This is done by cutting opposite bevels on either side of the window/ rectangle line, which is the same pencil line.

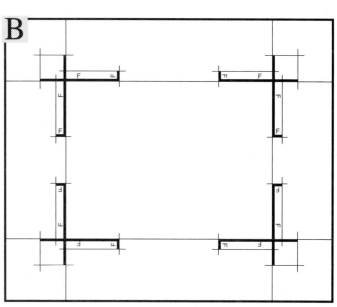

*Far cuts are cuts made farther, or beyond, the standard reach[1] of the dimensioning system. How this is done is explained in Step 6. For many of you this concept will not become clear until you actually do it. For this Extended Corners mat, there are <u>four</u> far cuts on each side.

[1] The standard reach of the 4501 dimensioning system is 6". The 4505 dimension system will reach out to 8".

Design: Extended Corners

Look at Diagrams B & C. The far cuts are indicated by the heavy lines marked "F". There are four at each corner — two of the long rectangle sides, two of the square's sides, and the two short rectangle ends **(Diagrams B & C)**. **Be sure to mark the "F's" exactly as shown.**

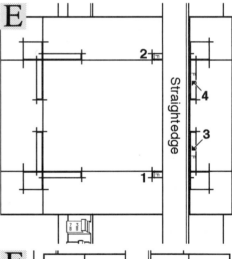

6 **Cut the far cuts, sixteen total.** Set the dimensioning system at 4-1/2" or 5" so as not to bend your mat, and slide the mat under the straightedge as shown. Line up the straightedge with your "F" reverse pencil lines. **When cutting the far cuts, the "F" and pencil lines should be showing and not covered by the straightedge.** For example: Line up <u>and</u> cut 1 and 2, being very careful not to over or undercut, **(Diagram D)**.

7 **Keeping the mat under the straightedge, pull the mat to the left until the straightedge lines up with lines 3 and 4 (Diagram E).** Rotate the mat to each of its four edges, at each side cutting two short rectangle ends and two long rectangle sides.

8 **Rotate mat 90° and repeat for each new side (Diagram F) for cuts 5, 6, 7, and 8.**

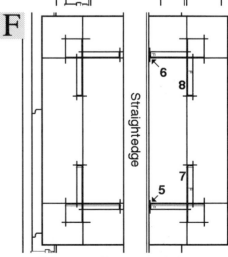

Design: Extended Corners

9 When <u>all</u> sixteen far cuts are made, put the dimensioning system back at 2-1/8". Cut out the other long sides of each rectangle. These cuts are made normally, not far cuts. The lines for these are marked with an "X" **(Diagram G)**. There will be eight cuts total. These cuts create the outside corner at the intersection of the rectangle and the square. Cut all the way into the square to make this corner. If the rectangle falls out, you have cut far enough.

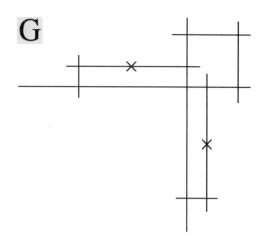

G

10 Now set the dimensioning system back at 1-1/2". Cut the outside two edges of each of the four corner squares (lines marked with an "X") **(Diagram H)**.

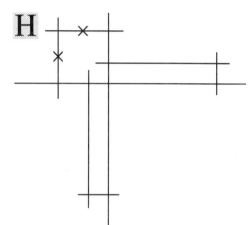

H

11 You need only cut out the mat's window to show whatever you are matting. To do this, set the dimensioning system back at 2-1/2" and cut as you would a plain, single-opening mat. Be careful not to overcut these lines. If you do, you will cut through the rectangles and lose them. Turn your mat over now and admire your impressive handiwork!

For added effect, make this a double mat (see 4501/4505 instructions, "Cutting a Double Mat" p. 10). Set the dimensioning system at 2-3/4", draw four reference lines (one on each side) and cut just as you would on any second mat. This will give you a 1/4" difference between the first and second mats.

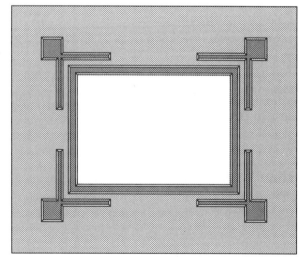

Once you understand how to cut this mat, you are ready to change the dimensions to fit what you are matting. Just make sure to draw the corner squares with the dimensioning system set an inch smaller than it was for your border width, and draw the rectangles with the dimensioning system set at 3/8" smaller than it was for your border width. You can also change the dimensions of the corner squares and connecting rectangles if you wish—just do everything in the same order, but use your chosen dimensions.

For an added design accent use mosaic squares (see 4501/4505 instructions, p. 16).

Photo Inset

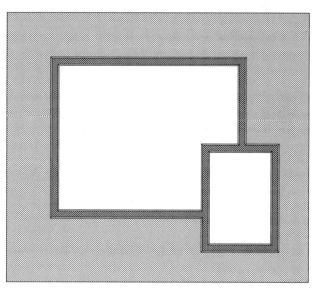

This mat is done in five stages. First, draw all lines on the back of the top mat and label the two far cut* reference lines. Second, cut the far cuts and the regular cuts. Third, attach a second piece of smaller matboard to the back of the first. Fourth, draw all lines on the back of the mat and label the three far cut reference lines. Fifth, cut the far cuts and the regular cuts. Learn this pattern on practice matboard first.

Materials: Alto's 4501 or 4505 Mat Cutting System. You will also need a piece of 14" x 16" matboard, a piece of 13-1/2" x 15-1/2" matboard, double-stick tape, a sharp cutting blade, and a very sharp pencil to draw all lines directly against the straightedge.

1 **Start with a 14" x 16" piece of matboard back side up and write "Top Mat" on an edge.** Set the dimensioning system to 1-5/8" and draw two reference lines as shown (**Diagram A**).

2 **Set the dimensioning system to 2-3/8".** Draw two reference lines in the opposite corner of Step 1 (**Diagram A**).

3 **Set the dimensioning system to 3-3/8".** Draw two additional reference lines as shown (**Diagram A**).

4 **Set the dimensioning system to 5-7/8".** Draw one reference line intersecting a <u>1-5/8" line</u> and a <u>3-3/8"</u> line, as shown (**Diagram B**).

Hint: A small plastic T-Square makes drawing these extra lines much easier. We paid 89¢ for one at a local crafts store.

5 **Using a ruler or a small 12" T-Square draw a reference line 6-3/4" in from the left edge, as shown (Diagram C).** Make sure this line is parallel to the left edge. Label the far cut reference lines with an "F" as shown.

* Far cuts are cuts made farther, or beyond, the standard reach[1] of the dimensioning system. How this is done is explained in Step 6. For many of you this concept will not become clear until you actually do it. For this Photo Inset mat, there are <u>two</u> far cuts on the top mat and <u>three</u> on the bottom mat.

[1] The standard reach of the 4501 dimensioning system is 6". The 4505 dimension system will reach out to 8".

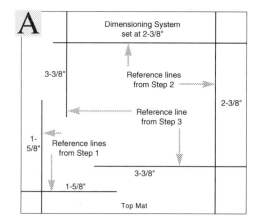

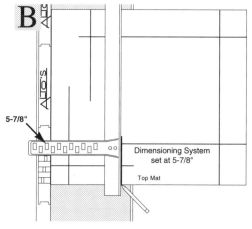

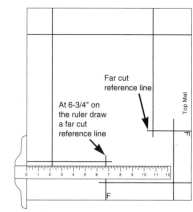

6 **Cut the first far cut (5-7/8").** Some of these cuts are farther from the outside edge than the system will reach, but this is easily overcome by raising the mat over the stops and lining up the reference line. This keeps the beveled angle correct for the opening. First, set the dimensioning system at 5" so as not to bend the matboard. Next, slide the mat under the straightedge and over the stops as shown. Stop as soon as the straightedge lines up with the "F" labeled far cut line. When it is perfectly lined up, cut (**Diagram D**). Start your cut an inch, or so, before the 3-3/8" line and stop on the stop reference line.

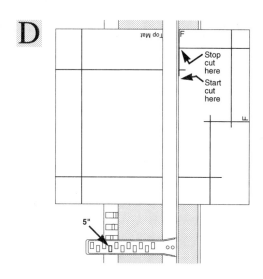

7 **Turn your mat clockwise 90°(no diagram).** Slide the mat under the straightedge and over the stops. Stop as soon as the straightedge lines up with the "F" labeled line. When it is perfectly lined up, cut. Start your cut on the start reference line (1-5/8") and stop your cut an inch, or so, past the 3-3/8" line.

8 **Set the dimensioning system to 1-5/8".** Cut the two short cuts from reference line to reference line (**Diagram E**).

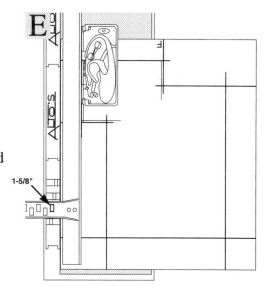

9 **Set the dimensioning system to 3-3/8".** Cut the two cuts. Here the outside corner cuts have to cross (**no diagram**).

10 **Set the dimensioning system to 2-3/8".** Cut the two remaining cuts (**no diagram**). The window scrap should fall out.

11 **DOUBLE MAT (see 4501/4505 instructions, p. 10).** First, cut another piece of matboard a little smaller than the top mat (approximately 13-1/2" x 15-1/2"). Replace the window piece on the top mat. Using double-stick tape attach the smaller bottom mat, face down to the back of the first mat as shown. Put a little tape on the window piece to adhere it to the second mat. Write "Bottom Mat" on an edge (**Diagram F**).

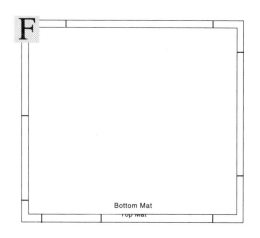

12 Set the dimensioning system to 2" and draw two reference lines as shown (**Diagram G**). These lines are in the same corner that had the 1-5/8" lines on the top mat.

13 Set the dimensioning system to 2-3/4". Draw two reference lines in the opposite corner of Step 12 (**Diagram G**).

14 Set the dimensioning system to 3-3/4". Draw two additional reference lines as shown (**Diagram G**).

15 Set the dimensioning system to 5-1/2". Draw a reference line intersecting the 2" line as shown. Label this line with an "F3" (upside-down) as shown (**Diagram G**).

16 Set the dimensioning system to 5-5/8". Draw a reference line right next to your previous line. <u>This line</u> forms the corner with the 3-3/4" line as shown (**Diagram G**).

17 Using a ruler draw a reference line 7" in from the <u>left edge of the TOP MAT</u>, as shown (**Diagram H**). This line completes the large window. Label this line with an upside-down "F2" <u>as shown</u>.

18 Using a ruler draw a reference line 7-1/8" in from the same <u>left edge of the TOP MAT</u>, as shown (**Diagram H**). This line completes the little window with the "F3" line. Label this line with a rightside-up "F1" as shown in **Diagram H**.
To prevent starting or stopping on the wrong line when cutting, it helps to have your reference lines look like **Detail H**.

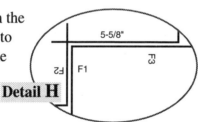

Detail H

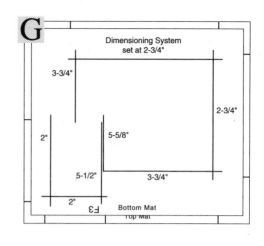

G

Dimensioning System
set at 2-3/4"

3-3/4"

2-3/4"

2"

5-5/8"

5-1/2"

3-3/4"

2"

F3

Bottom Mat
Top Mat

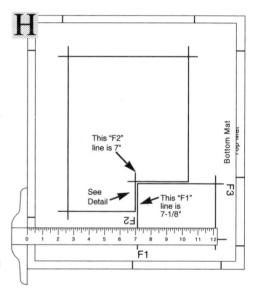

H

This "F2"
line is 7"

See
Detail

This "F1"
line is
7-1/8"

Bottom Mat

F3

F2

F1

19 Cut the wide border cut labeled "F1". Set the dimensioning system at 5" so as not to bend the matboard. Slide the mat under the straightedge and over the stops as shown. Stop as soon as the straightedge lines up with the "F1" labeled line. The "F1" is rightside-up. When it is perfectly lined up, cut (**Diagram I**). Start your cut on the 2" start reference line and stop your cut on the "F3" stop reference line – <u>NOT the 5-5/8" line</u>.

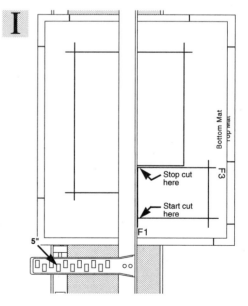

I

Bottom Mat

F3

Stop cut
here

Start cut
here

F1

5"

Design: Photo Inset

20 Cut the wide border cut labeled "F2". Rotate your matboard 180°. Keep the dimensioning system at 5". Slide the mat under the straightedge and over the stops. Stop as soon as the straightedge lines up with the "F2" line. The "F2" is rightside-up. When it is perfectly lined up, cut (**Diagram J**). Start your cut an inch, or so, before the 5-5/8" line and stop on the 3-3/4" stop reference line.

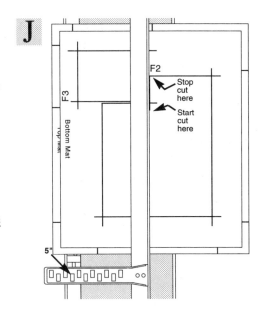

21 Cut the wide border cut labeled "F3" (no diagram). Rotate your matboard clockwise 90°. When it is perfectly lined up, cut. <u>Start your cut on the "F1" start reference line</u> and stop your cut on the 2" stop reference line.

22 Set the dimensioning system to 5-5/8" (no diagram). Cut from the 3-3/4" start reference line to about an inch past the "F2" line. The outside corner cuts have to cross.

23 Set the dimensioning system to 3-3/4" (no diagram). Very carefully cut the two cuts from reference line to reference line – "F2" to 2-3/4", and 2-3/4" to 5-5/8".

24 Set the dimensioning system to 2" (no diagram). Cut the two short cuts – "F3" to 2", and 2" to "F1".

25 Set the dimensioning system to 2-3/4". Cut the two remaining cuts (**Diagram K**). The window scraps should fall out.

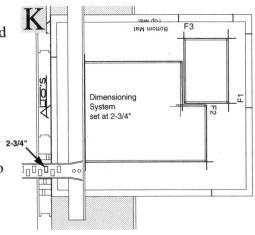

Carefully trim your photos and attach.

Many variations of this mat are possible. A diploma with the proud recipient's photo in a corner looks great. Other suggestions are a large photo of your teenager and a small photo of the same person as a young child, or school and team pictures, etc.

Oval with a Freehand Accent

Focus on EACH cut to see: – where is the START – where is the STOP – then, and only then, cut.

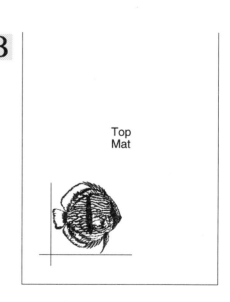

*T*o succeed in cutting this fancy mat, you need experience in freehand cutting and in cutting double oval mats (Alto's Oval Templates instructions, p. 10). You can **practice** cutting freehand designs with the Model 30 mat cutter, included with the oval templates, on matboard scraps until you feel comfortable with the process (see Oval instructions, p. 14).

All cutting and reference lines for this mat will be done on the front of the matboard. Therefore, to make sure that erasing won't damage or discolor your matboard, start by drawing a test line on the front of a scrap of the actual matboard you are using and erase with a plastic eraser. Always draw with pencil very lightly so as not to dent the matboard, and for ease of erasing. The first time you cut this mat, start with a *simple* freehand cut **and practice, practice, practice**.

   Materials: Alto's Oval Template Set. You will also need two pieces of 11" x 14" matboard, double-stick tape, a non-abrasive eraser, a sharp cutting blade, and a pencil.

1 **Select two pieces of 11" x 14" matboard, making sure that they are exactly the same size so that they align perfectly.** For your reference, lightly label on the front center of each which will be the top mat, and which the bottom mat.

2 **Set the dimensioning system of the Alto's 4501 or 4505 System at 1-5/8", or use a ruler.** Put the top matboard in under the straightedge, front side up and lightly draw two intersecting reference lines in what will be the bottom left corner of the mat **(Diagram A)**. **Do the same to the bottom piece of matboard.**

A

> Top
> Mat
>
> Dimensioning System
> set at 1-5/8"

3 **Using a large or medium sized stamp, a stencil, or a template, stamp or draw your image on the top mat, carefully placing it in the bottom left corner within the intersecting lines you drew in Step 2 (Diagram B).** When using a wooden-backed rubber stamp, carefully line up the corner edges of the wood part of the stamp with your intersecting corner lines, for ease of alignment later. Be sure to let the stamp ink dry completely to avoid smearing. Don't worry about the stamp quality at this time, only the placement. This stamp is just a guide, not the one that will show on the finished mat.

The stamp we used for our example here is "Tropical Fish 2" Jumbo Stamp #2386 by Comotion Decorative Rubber Stamp of Tucson, AZ 602-889-2200.

B

> Top
> Mat

4 Using a sharp pencil, lightly trace around the stamp image, <u>staying about 1/4" from the edge of the image</u>. Get as detailed as you wish, but detail will make the freehand cut more difficult **(Diagram C)**.

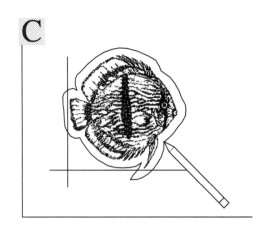

C

5 Place a scrap matboard cutting surface under the mat and cut around your image on the pencil lines you just drew. Always have your stamp image to the left of your cut so that the bevel will show the mat's core: ⬛⬛⬛ ⬛⬛⬛ not ⬛⬛⬛ ⬛⬛⬛ (side views). **Don't try to do this step in one continuous cut.** Instead, start and stop and restart the cut as often as necessary. Cut carefully and smoothly along the pencil lines **(Diagram D)**.

Detail D

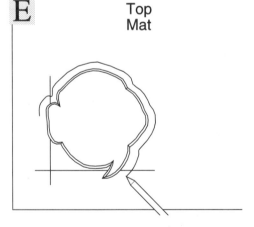

D

6 Lightly draw another pencil line around the fish, this time 1/4" inch from the edge of the freehand cut you just made. You don't need to trace all the way around the fish, as the bottom section of line will just be erased **(Diagram E)**.

7 Carefully align the two pieces of matboard, top piece on top. Place on a scrap matboard cutting surface. Make sure that the intersecting 2" lines (on the bottom matboard) and the freehand cut (on the top matboard) are both in the bottom left corner.

E

Top Mat

8 Remove the bottom tack from the No. 3 oval template and place the template on the front of the aligned mats so that the fish (or whatever image you are using) is under the oval **(Diagram F)**. Pound the three remaining tacks in, making sure they go through both mats.

9 Remove the template and set the bottom mat aside. Reposition the template on the top mat, fitting the tacks into the existing tack holes. Pound the tacks into place.

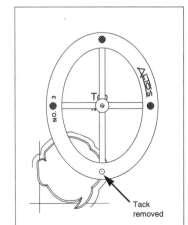

F

Tack removed

Design: Oval with Freehand Accent

10 **Place the 1/4" spacer on the cutting tool and cut the oval opening.** Use the line you drew 1/4" outside your freehand cut fish as the start and stop lines for your cut **(Diagram G)**. <u>**Do not** cut the oval all the way to the freehand cut so that it falls out.</u> To begin the oval cuts with a smooth blade entry, start by setting the cutting tool on the mat with the guide points against the template and the blade point just resting on the mat. Now, gently sink the blade into the matboard on the start line at the angle it is pointing, so as not to break the blade tip. When the blade is completely inserted, both guide points on the cutter should still be against the template. You are now ready to move the cutter forward against the template. When you have reached the stop line, remove the cutter and carefully pull the template from the matboard.

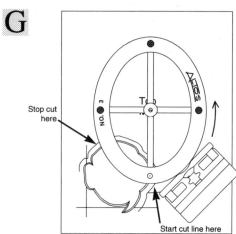

G

11.1 **Replace the window scrap of the stamped image.** Before cutting see Step 11.2. Freehand cut the remainder of the mat's opening by cutting along the section of the line labeled "CUT THIS LINE" **(Diagram H)**.

H

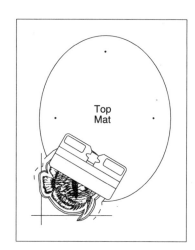

11.2 **Be aware of the bevel direction.** You want the mat's core to show, so <u>the mat's oval opening</u>, not the fish this time, will be to the <u>left of the blade as you cut</u> **(Diagram I)**. Be careful to *avoid overcuts*. Gently erase any pencil lines on the matboard, including the 1-5/8" intersecting lines from Step 2.

I

12 **Carefully align the two mats with the top mat on top.** Make sure that the intersecting 1-5/8" lines (on the bottom matboard) and the freehand cut (on the top matboard) are <u>both in the bottom left corner</u>. Holding the mats in place, draw another light pencil line on the bottom mat, <u>1/4" from the freehand cut</u> you just made in Step 11 **(Diagram J)**. **Set the finished top mat aside.**

J

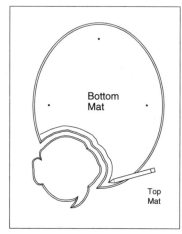

Design: Oval with Freehand Accent

13 Position the No. 3 oval (with bottom tack removed) on the bottom mat, fitting the three tacks into the tack holes you made before. Pound the tacks in place. Without the spacer, use the cutting tool to cut out the oval opening, again using the pencil line you drew in Step 12 as your start and stop lines (**Diagram K**). Carefully pull the template from the matboard.

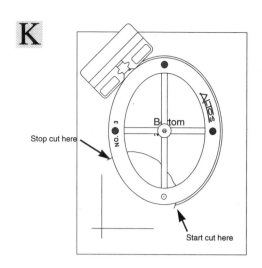

14 Finish freehand cutting the bottom mat's opening by cutting along the pencil line labeled "CUT THIS LINE." This is the same pencil line you drew in Step 12 (**Diagram L**). The window piece will fall out.

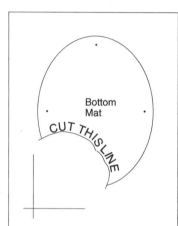

15 Now stamp your image again in the lower left corner of the bottom mat. Line up the edges of the wooden stamp with the pencil lines (as you did with the top mat), so that your image will be perfectly placed in the freehand cut when the top mat is added (**Diagram M**). This is the image that shows, so stamp carefully. **Let the ink dry completely before gently erasing any pencil lines.**

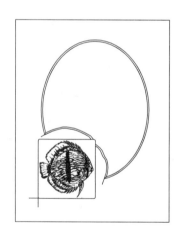

16 Stick the finished mats together with double-stick tape. Because we carefully lined up the two mats at each step, the two oval cuts and the freehand cuts should be perfectly lined up when the mats are put together (**Diagram N**).

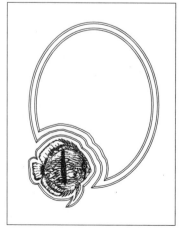

Once you have mastered these techniques, you can experiment by using different stamp images, drawings, or even objects affixed to the mat (such as feathers, leaves, small ceramic masks, coins, etc.) The window opening can be rectangular as well as oval, or any other shape you desire. It is important when cutting both your freehand image and the oval or other-shaped opening, to always stay at least an inch from the edge of the matboard. Cutting too close will cause the mat to bend or interfere with framing.

Design: Oval with Freehand Accent

Raised Accents

This mat is done in three stages. First, you will cut a single window mat. Second, cut the raised bevel accents. Third, glue the raised accents to the front of the single mat.

Materials: Alto's 4501 or 4505 Mat Cutting System. You will also need two pieces of 11" x 14" matboard, a sharp cutting blade, some glue, and a sharp pencil.

1 **Begin with an 11" x 14" piece of matboard <u>face down</u> and set the system at 2-1/2".** With a sharp pencil, draw start/stop lines on the back side of the matboard on all four sides **(Diagram A)**.

A

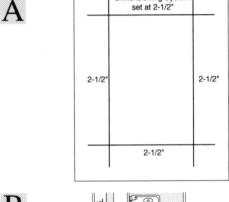

2 **Make cuts on all four sides of the matboard.** The window should fall out. Set the single mat aside **(no diagram)**.

Now you will cut a series of parallel strips as the raised accents. To get the bevels right, half the cuts will be from the top.

3 **Place the other piece of matboard <u>face down</u>, with the 14" edge against the stops.** Set the system at 2". Make a cut approximately 1" from the bottom edge to approximately 1" from the top edge as illustrated **(Diagram B)**.

B

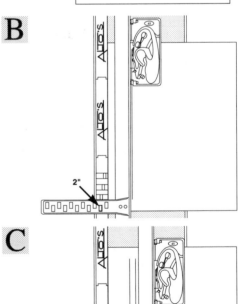

4 **Move the cutting guide to the right, one hole, so the system is set at 2-1/2".** Make a cut approximately 1" from the bottom edge to approximately 1" from the top edge **(no diagram)**.

5 **Move the cutting guide to the right, three holes so the system is set at 4".** Make a cut approximately 2" from the bottom edge to approximately 2" from the top edge as illustrated **(Diagram C)**.

C

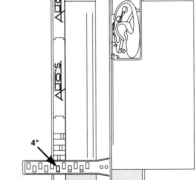

6 **Move the cutting guide to the right, one hole so the system is set at 4-1/2".** Make a cut approximately 2" from the bottom edge to approximately 2" from the top edge **(no diagram)**.

Design: Raised Accents

7 Turn the matboard <u>face up</u>. Set the system at 4-1/4", as shown. Make a cut approximately 2" from the bottom edge to approximately 2" from the top edge (**Diagram D**).

8 Move the cutting guide to the left one hole so the system is set at 3-3/4". Make a cut similar to Step 7 (**no diagram**).

9 Move the cutting guide to the left three holes so the system is set at 2-1/4". Make a cut similar to Step 7 (**no diagram**).

10 Move the cutting guide to the left one hole so the system is set at 1-3/4". Make a cut similar to Step 7 (**no diagram**).

11 Turn the matboard 90°, as shown. Set the measuring system to 2-1/2". Make a cut over the first four long cuts, cutting the ends of the long strips (**Diagram E**).

12 Turn the matboard 180° so the other 11" edge is against the stops. Keep the system at 2-1/2" and cut out the long strips (**no diagram**). Three pieces should fall out. Keep the two pieces that have the bevel on the same top side all the way around. Discard the other piece.

13 Set the system at 4". Make a cut over the four remaining strips (**Diagram F**).

14 Turn the matboard 180°. Leave the system at 4". Cut out the short strips (**no diagram**). Three pieces should fall out. Keep the two pieces that have the bevel on the same top side all the way around. Discard the other piece. You should now have four raised accent pieces: two of them are 9" long and the other two are 6" long.

15 Turn the matboard over so it is <u>face down</u>, with the 11" edge against the stops. Set the system at 3-1/2". Make a cut over the four cuts of the smaller opening (**no diagram**). Discard the three small pieces that fall out. This step makes a reverse bevel for two of your square accent pieces cut in Step 17.

16 Turn the matboard 180°. Repeat Step 15 (**no diagram**).

17 Turn the matboard <u>face up</u>, with the 11" edge against the stops. Set the system back two posts to 3-1/4" (**Diagram G**). Cut off the ends of the strips to make two small square accent pieces. Keep the two squares that have the bevel on the same top side all the way around. Discard the other piece.

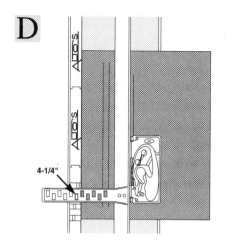

D

4-1/4"

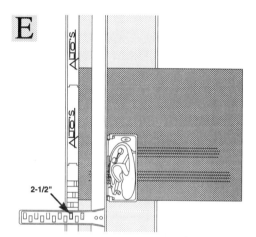

E

2-1/2"

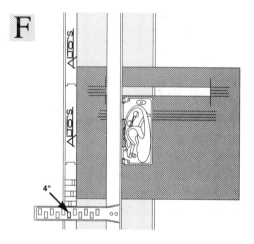

F

4"

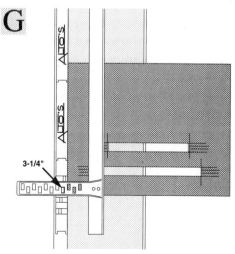

G

3-1/4"

Design: Raised Accents

18 Turn the matboard 180°. Repeat Step 17 for two more square accent pieces (no diagram).

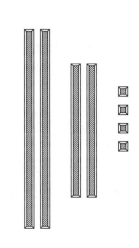

You should now have one single window mat (not shown here), two longer thin rectangles, two shorter thin rectangles and four small squares (Diagram H).

Do the next steps with care and patience. When gluing, rubber cement is the safest, as it can be wiped off. White glue is a more permanent adhesive. However, it will stain if it touches the mat or oozes out from under the decorative strips.

19 Place the single window mat against the stops <u>face up</u> on a 14" side. Set the system to 1-3/4". Apply glue to one of your long rectangular accent pieces. <u>Use only tiny amounts of glue to avoid any squeezing out of excess</u> (Diagram I).

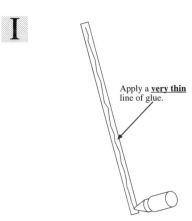

Apply a **very thin** line of glue.

20 Using the cutting guide as an aid, glue the raised accent pieces onto the face of the mat. Match the longer accents to the longer sides, etc. (Diagram J).

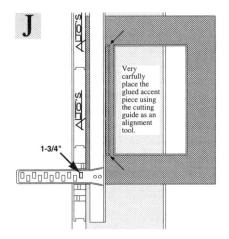

Very carfully place the glued accent piece using the cutting guide as an alignment tool.

1-3/4"

21 When the longer accents are in place, glue one small square in each corner (Diagram K).

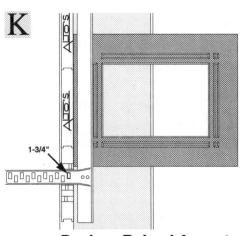

1-3/4"

Now that you have successfully cut this mat, try it for artwork of your own. Experiment with the shapes and sizes of the accent pieces, how they are arranged, and/or the color of the accent pieces. Using white matboard with white core and the same color of accent pieces provides a very elegant, embossed looking mat. A white mat in black core, with black core accents is also very striking.

Design: Raised Accents

Stepped Arced Corners

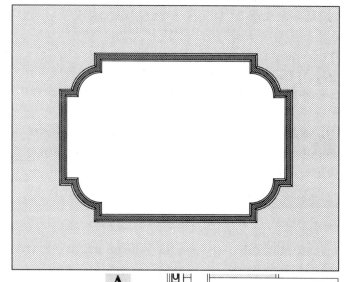

*T*his impressive mat is simple and quick, but accuracy is *vital*.

When making reference lines, use a sharp, fine-point pencil directly against the straightedge, and make sure the matboard is always snug against the stops. Push the Model 360 tack <u>precisely</u> through the center of the reference **+**'s. Even small errors can throw off the circle cuts visibly, but with attentiveness to these suggestions, success is assured.

The mat is created in four stages. First, draw all reference lines on the back of the top mat. Second, use the Model 360 to cut the circle cuts on the <u>front</u> of the matboard. Third, cut the straight cuts on the <u>back</u> of the matboard. Fourth and last, repeat the entire process on the bottom mat with a 1/4" difference in measurements.

Materials: Alto's Model 360 Circle Cutter, and a 4501 or 4505 Mat Cutting System. You will also need two pieces of 11" x 14" matboard, sharp cutting blades, and a sharp pencil. Use two different shades of 11" x 14" matboard, *making sure the two pieces are exactly the same size.* Unlike other double mats, this one does **not** require cutting the bottom mat down in size.

1 **Set the dimensioning system at 2" and place what will be the <u>top</u> mat under the straightedge.** Draw the reference lines for each of the four sides of the window opening **(Diagram A)**.

2 **Add 1-1/2" to the first setting, moving the arms over three holes.** The dimensioning system will now be set at 3-1/2". Draw two lines in each corner to form stepped corners as shown **(Diagram B)**.

3 **Add 1/4" to the last setting, moving the arms up two posts.** The dimensioning system is now set at 3-3/4". Draw two short, intersecting lines in each corner as shown **(Diagram C)**. These will be the reference **+**'s for the Model 360 circle cuts.

Focus on EACH cut to see: – where is the START – where is the STOP – then, and only then, cut.

Design: Stepped Arced Corners

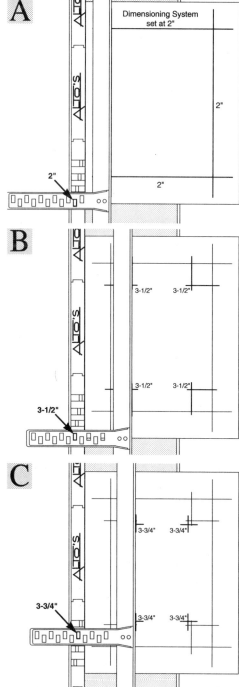

4 Erase the extra lines in all four corners until you have only the lines as shown in Diagram D.

5 Very carefully align the top and bottom mats together, so that they are perfectly lined up (no diagram).

6 Remove the centering tack from the Model 360. Push it through the center of each of the four +'s you drew in Step 3, pushing through <u>both</u> the top and bottom mat at the same time (**Diagram D**)*.

7 After the holes have been punched, separate the two pieces of matboard and set the bottom mat aside (no diagram).

8 Place the centering tack in the arm of the Model 360 in the hole marked 2-1/2".

9 Flip the top matboard over to the <u>front side</u> and reinsert the centering tack (still in the Model 360 arm) into the tack hole. Push the tack through both the top mat you are working on <u>and</u> a scrap piece underneath, to anchor it firmly before you cut (**Diagram E**).

10 Lower the blade into the <u>front</u> of the matboard and cut a 3/4 circle crescent in each corner of the mat (**Diagram F**). Do not cut the circle all the way out. You are only making sure you cut all the way through the corner.

11 Turn the matboard over, <u>face down</u>. The heavy line represents the minimum where you should have cut all the way through the matboard (**Diagram G**).

* If you have difficulties pushing the tack through two pieces of matboard at the same time, try pushing the tack through the +'s on just the top matboard, skipping Steps 5 & 7. After you have drawn the stepped corner lines on the bottom mat in Step 15, push the tack through the intersection of the stepped corner and continue with Step 16.

D

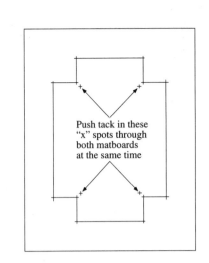

Push tack in these "x" spots through both matboards at the same time

E

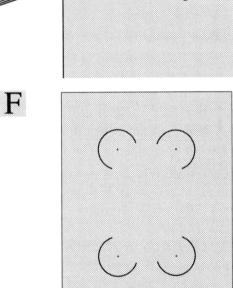

Front side of mat showing

F

Front side of mat showing

G

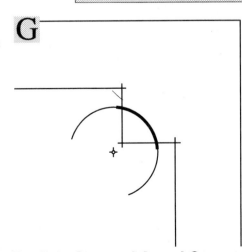

Design: Stepped Arced Corners

12 Place the matboard face down in the dimensioning system, set at 3-1/2". On the back of the mat, cut the eight short lines which connect the circle cuts to the reference lines of the window opening – cuts made in this step are indicated by heavy lines **(Diagram H)**. Use the 2" window opening reference lines as precise start/stop lines for these cuts, and cut <u>past</u> the circle cut line.

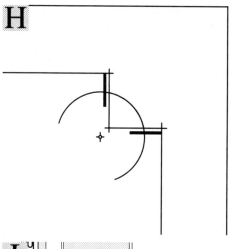

13 Set the dimensioning system at 2". Make the four long cuts of the window opening, using the pencil lines drawn for the stepped corners as start/stop lines **(Diagrams I & J)**. The window piece should now fall out.

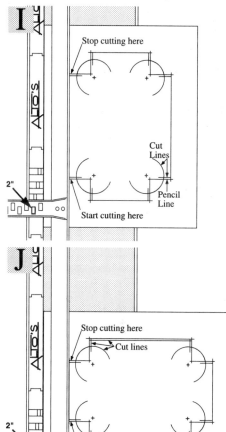

Now we will repeat Steps 1-13 (except for Step 3, 5 & 7) on what will be the bottom matboard, with 1/4" difference in measurements (1/4" is an attractive difference between the top mat and liner).

14 Set the dimensioning system at 2-1/4" and place what will be the <u>bottom</u> mat under the straightedge. Draw the reference lines for each of the four sides of the window opening **(similar to Diagram A)**.

15 Set the dimensioning system at 3-3/4". Draw two lines in each corner to form stepped corners as shown **(Diagram K)**. These lines will be drawn lines over the holes you punched in Step 6.

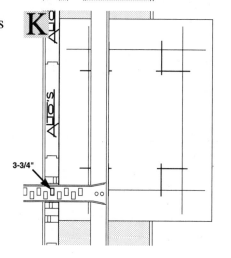

Design: Stepped Arced Corners

16 Erase the extra lines in all four corners until you have only the lines shown. There should be holes in the four intersections of the stepped corners (**Diagram L**).

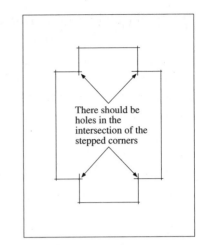

There should be holes in the intersection of the stepped corners

17 Place the centering tack in the arm of the Model 360 in the hole marked 2".

18 Flip the matboard over to the front side and reinsert the centering tack (still in the Model 360 arm) into the tack hole. Push the tack through both the bottom mat you are working on <u>and</u> the scrap piece to anchor it firmly before you cut (**Diagram M**).

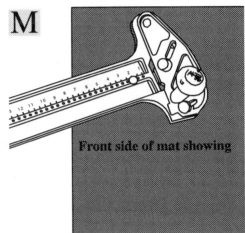

Front side of mat showing

19 Lower the blade into the front of the matboard and cut three fourths of a circle in each corner of the mat (similar to **Diagram F**). Do not cut the circle all the way out – only make sure you cut all the way through the corner.

20 Turn the matboard over, face down. Make sure you have cut all the way through the corners drawn on the back (see the heavy line of **Diagram G**).

21 Place the matboard face down in the dimensioning system, set at 3-3/4". On the back of the mat, cut the eight short lines which connect the circle cuts to the reference lines of the window opening. Cuts made in this step are indicated by heavy lines (**Diagram N**). Use the 2-1/4" window opening reference lines as precise start/stop lines for these cuts, and cut <u>past</u> the circle cut line.

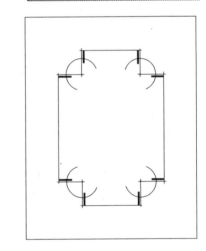

22 Set the dimensioning system at 2-1/4". Make the four long cuts of the window opening, using the pencil lines drawn for the stepped corners as start/stop lines (**Diagram O**). The window piece should now fall out.

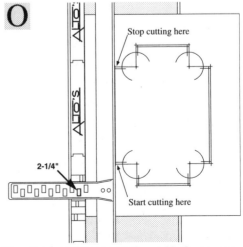

Stop cutting here

2-1/4"

Start cutting here

23 Double-stick tape the bottom mat to the back of the top mat, lining up the edges perfectly.

As always, when you become comfortable with this mat, you can change the measurements to fit your art.

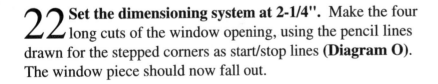

Design: Stepped Arced Corners

Fabric Covered Mat

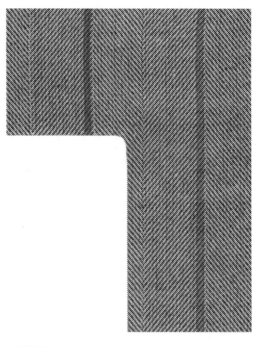

This versatile technique allows as many varieties of mats as there are workable fabrics, and greatly expands your framing options. Use a natural fabric such as cotton or rayon. (Polyester can be difficult to glue.) Fabrics that are too heavy are difficult to wrap. Fuzzy, stretchy, linty, or fraying fabrics are not recommended. Always test your fabric first by gluing a scrap of it to scrap matboard to determine if it will adhere properly. Press the fabric thoroughly before you begin. Following these instructions will result in a mat perfectly sized for a 5" x 7" photograph or art card.

Materials: Alto's 4501 or 4505 Mat Cutting System, a 12" x 14" piece of fabric, a 9" x 11" matboard, a razor blade, a neutral Ph adhesive such as *Lineco's* White Neutral Polyvinyl/Acetate (PVA).

1 **Cut matboard to 9" x 11".** Use white matboard or the white backside of any scrap matboard. Darker colors may show through thin or light-colored fabrics.

2 **Set the dimensioning system of the 4501 or 4505 to 2-1/8" and draw four reference lines on the back of the mat, one on each side of the mat (Diagram A).**

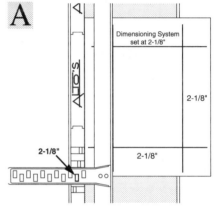

3 **Cut all four sides of the mat, using the start/stop reference lines you just drew.** This mat will crop your art or photograph 1/8" on all sides.

4 **Lay the pressed fabric face down on a clean cutting surface** (scrap matboard works well). Lay your mat on the fabric and trim the fabric to 1" larger than the mat on all sides as shown **(Diagram B)**. You can use a razor blade to do this. If your fabric is striped, be sure to cut parallel to the stripes so they are not crooked.

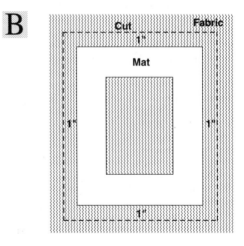

5 **Remove the mat and apply glue to the white side of the mat** (this will be the front of the finished mat). Use glue sparingly, as too much will soak through the fabric and show on the front (the thinner the fabric, the greater the chance of this). Spread glue evenly over the entire mat surface **(Diagram C)**. Leaving spots uncovered with adhesive can result in fabric "bubbles." If you are using a very thin or sheer fabric, blot the spread glue with a piece of craft paper.

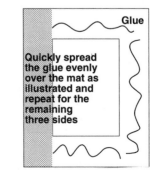

Design: Fabric Covered Mat

6 Lay the mat, glue side down, in the middle of the <u>back side</u> of your fabric so that 1" of fabric sticks out on each side as shown (Diagram D). If you are using a striped fabric, make sure the edges of the mat line up exactly with the stripes in your fabric as you lay the mat down. Press the mat onto the fabric. Flip the mat and fabric over and use your hands to smooth the fabric onto the mat from the front side. With some glues and fabrics, you may find it helpful to let the glue dry before you proceed to each next step.

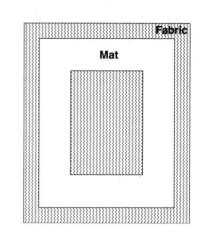

D

7 Spread glue as you did before on the back side of the mat on one edge, to 1" from the outside edge as shown. Carefully and snugly pull the fabric around one edge of the mat and adhere to the back of the mat (**Diagram E**). Press and smooth with your hand on the back and then on front of the mat.

8 Repeat Step 7 on the edge <u>opposite</u> the one you just completed.

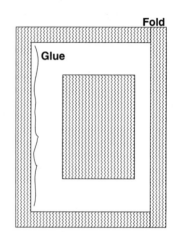

E

9 Before you fold the last two sides, trim the four corners of fabric as shown, to within 1/4" of the corner of the matboard (**Diagram F**). Then trim off the flap shown in **Detail F1** so it looks like **Detail F2**. This will lessen fabric bulk and aid adhesion, especially for heavier fabrics. If you cut any closer than 1/4", your corners may fray and show on the front.

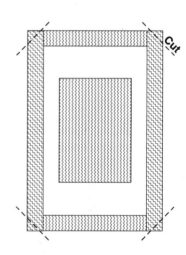

F

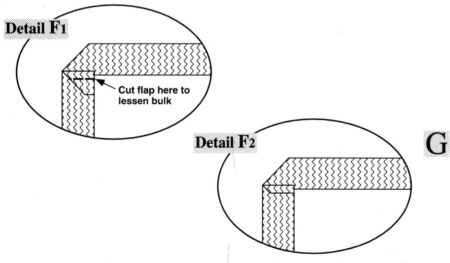

Detail F1

Cut flap here to lessen bulk

Detail F2

G

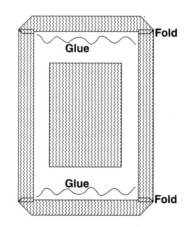

10 Repeat Step 7 for the remaining two sides of the mat (Diagram G).

Design: Fabric Covered Mat

11 Using a razor blade, cut a window out of the middle of the fabric, 1" from the mat window opening as shown (Diagram H).

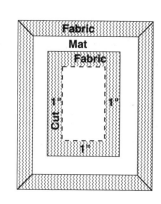

12 Cut on the four dashed lines as shown in Diagram I, from the inside corners of the fabric window opening to around 1/8" from the inside corners of the matboard window opening (closer for less stretchy fabrics and further for flimsy or stretchier fabrics). Don't cut all the way to the mat corners as fraying may occur. The fabric will stretch to compensate for that 1/8". Fabric-wrapped mats will not have sharp corners like paper mats. Fabric is soft and somewhat bulky, and you should expect more rounded corners, depending on the heaviness of the fabric.

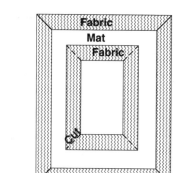

13 One side at a time, glue the four inside fabric tabs to the back of the mat. Spread glue evenly on the back of the matboard to 1" from one of the edges of the window opening, and snugly stretch the fabric tab around onto the glue (Diagram J). Smooth toward the outside edges of the mat with your fingers.

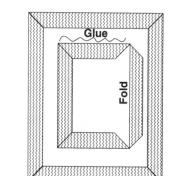

14 When all four flaps of Step 13 are glued, flip the mat over and press the front flat with your hands (no diagram).

15 Turn over to the back and dab a bit of glue on the back of each inside corner to prevent fraying (Diagram K). Be careful not to let glue show on the front of the mat.

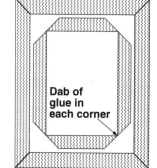

As the glue dries, some warping of the matboard may occur.

This technique can be used to cover old mats that are already cut. Covering mats with the bevel up gives you a softer, rounder corner, good with heavy fabrics; while covering mats with the bevel down gives a sharper edge, good with thinner fabrics.

Preservation: Use acid-free white glue and/or neutral pH adhesives. Since fabrics are bleached, scoured, and dyed, it is wise to insert a buffer of 4-ply acid free cotton ragboard between the fabric mat and your art. This is true for all fabrics, even natural fibers.

Design: Fabric Covered Mat

Shadow Box

The shadow box is ideal for displaying photos, buttons, heirlooms, wedding objects, coins, jewelry, christening gowns, graduation tassels and memorabilia. These instructions will result in a shadow box almost one inch deep with a 6-1/2" x 9" opening. It can be made using all one color of matboard, or with a different color background than the front mat color.

Materials: Alto's 4501 or 4505 Mat Cutting System, a 2" strip of matboard (see 4501/4505 instructions, p. 13), two pieces of 11" x 14" matboard, a sharp pencil, tape, double-stick tape or other adhesive, ruler, a fresh cutting blade, clean hands. For preservation, use acid-free tape, glue, and matboard. For accuracy, use a very sharp pencil and draw all lines with sharpened tip directly against the straightedge.

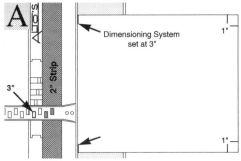

1 Place the 2" strip of matboard in the dimensioning system snug against the stops and set the dimensioning system at 3". Place what will be the background piece of 11" x 14" matboard (the box) <u>front side down</u> under the straightedge and against the non-beveled edge of the 2" strip. Draw two short reference marks on the back in each of the four corners as shown (**Diagram A**).

2 Remove the 2" strip, set the dimensioning system at 2", and draw four reference lines, again on the back side of the same matboard (Diagram B).

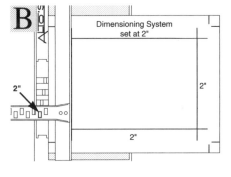

3 Set the dimensioning system at 2-1/8", and draw two short, crossing reference lines in each of the four corners of the reference lines you drew in Step 2, making four **+**'s (Diagram C).

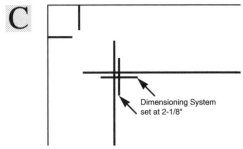

4 Using a ruler, draw two lines from the center point of the **+**'s drawn in Step 3, one to each of the two short reference lines drawn in Step 1 (Diagram D). Repeat for all four corners (eight lines total). These will be <u>actual</u> cut lines, not the reference lines you are used to drawing.

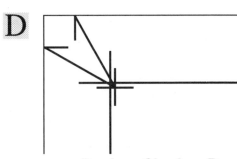

Steps 5-10 must be followed exactly so that the bevels will be in the correct direction for folding the box.

5 Set the dimensioning system at 5-1/8". Slide the mat diagonally under the cutting guide, and line the cutting guide up perfectly with one of the lines you drew in Step 4. Do <u>exactly</u> as shown in **Diagram E**, using the line at the top (line 1). At this point you may want to use a utility knife and cut on the angled lines to cut out the triangle pieces, but using Steps 5 through 10 should provide you with cleaner corners when assembling your shadow box.

6 Before cutting, hold the mat steady with your hand where indicated in Diagram E and without letting the matboard move, set the dimensioning system to 5". Place the cutter against the cutting guide as shown in **Diagram F**, and sink the blade tip through the matboard at the + center point, cutting all the way through the edge of the matboard on the line drawn in Step 4. For the piece to fall out easily later, sink the blade 1/16" before the + center point. This is only important if you want to use these pieces later to decorate the finished shadow box. If you cut more than 1/16" before the +, it will show in your finished shadow box.

7 Repeat Steps 5 and 6 three more times, turning the mat a quarter turn each time to cut lines 2, 3, and 4 as shown **(Diagrams E and F)**. You will always be cutting the right line of the pair of lines drawn in each corner in Step 4. Remember to return the dimensioning system to 5-1/8" to line up, then back to 5" for each cut. Now only four of the eight lines are cut. We'll cut the remaining four lines drawn in Step 4, but from a starting point different from that used for the first four cuts.

8 Set the dimensioning system at 5-1/8" and carefully line the cutting guide up with the pencil line as shown (Diagram G).

9 This time you will be cutting *from the mat's edge to the center point of the* + (Diagram H). It is important to cut in this direction to get the bevel facing correctly. As before, hold the mat in place and move the dimensioning system back to 5" before cutting. Cut on the line from the mat's edge until the blade has reached the center point of the +. The blade must be lowered before you begin cutting from the mat edge, so that the corner piece will fall out. When starting a cut with the cutter base partially off the edge, you may need to lean forward on the cutter a little to keep the blade down at the proper depth. If you plan to use the corner pieces, cut to just a hair past the center of the +.

10 Cut the remaining three lines by repeating Steps 8 and 9 after turning the mat a quarter turn after each cut **(Diagrams G and H)**. The corner pieces should fall out.

Design: Shadow Box

11 Raise the blade depth on the cutter so that it will cut almost all the way through the matboard but not quite. (You will be scoring the mat to fold, so the deeper you cut without cutting through, the sharper and cleaner your fold line will look.) To raise the blade, screw the blade depth screw clockwise (see 4501/4505 instructions, p. 2). Test on a scrap piece of the matboard you're using to determine the proper setting.

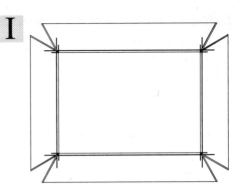

12 Set the dimensioning system to 2". Cut four lines on the same matboard back, using the start/stop reference lines drawn in Step 2. Be sure to ignore the v-cuts you just made and use the reference lines to start and stop the cuts (**Diagram I**).

Before the next step, clean the pencil graphite from the flat underside of the cutting tool with a damp paper towel, being careful not to cut yourself, and let it dry.

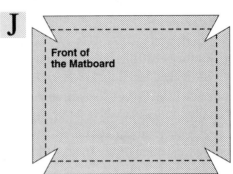

13 Set the dimensioning system at 3" and place the 2" strip under the cutting guide and against the stops as in Step 1. Flip the scored matboard over to the front side, place it snug against the strip, and cut from one v-opening to the next on all four sides (**Diagram J**). With darker matboard, don't press down heavily on the cutter, as the bottom of it will buff the matboard shiny.

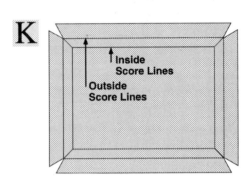

14 Place the mat front side down on a table and fold the four inside score lines (**Diagram K**) around a table edge. Flip it over and fold the four outside score lines in the opposite direction.

15 On the back side, put tape on one edge of the v-cut. Now, while looking at the front, tape the corner together, overlapping a tad to get a nice clean corner (**Diagram L**). Tape all four corners. Now you have an angled box with four flaps. Set the box aside.

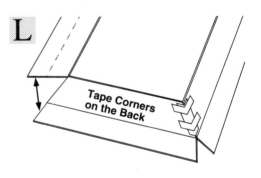

Set your cutter blade to the previous setting, to cut all the way through the matboard. Remove the 2" strip.

16 Set the dimensioning system to 2". Place the second piece of matboard under the cutting guide, front side down, and draw four reference lines on the back as shown (**Diagram M**). This will be the front mat of your shadow box.

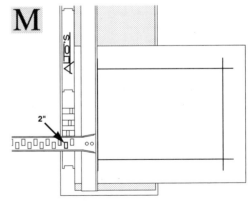

17 Cut all four sides, using the start/stop reference lines you just drew. The window opening should fall out.

Design: Shadow Box

18 Put double-stick tape or other adhesive on the four flaps of the box, and carefully lower the mat you just cut (front side up) onto the adhesive-covered flaps of the box (**Diagram N**). Look straight down onto the mat and not at an angle while doing this, to properly line up the bottom square of the box with the mat window opening (they are the same size). You have only one opportunity to center it properly. Another method to help you line up the two mats is to use the 2" strip and mark half lines on the back of the mat cut in Step 17 and lower the shadow box onto the cut mat. If you would like, the corner pieces can now be glued in the corners of the box or on the front mat to decorate (**Diagram O**). Your shadow box is ready to display!

By varying your measurements, you may make the box deeper or shallower, and vary the outer dimensions.

To attach objects to the inside of the shadow box, it is best to sew the object to the matboard, using a button on the back to reinforce (**Diagram P**). Clear silicone will work if the object cannot be sewn, but silicone is not reversible.

N

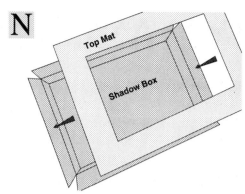

O

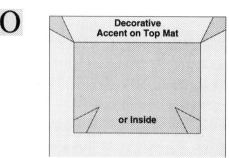

P

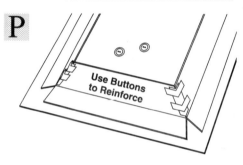

The same shadow box may be used for different objects. Before you assemble the shadow box, cut an opening in the bottom. Use the shadow box pattern you just learned and try this variation.

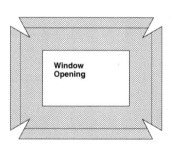

Cut the window center.

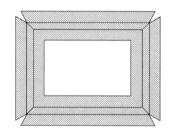

Assemble the shadow box.

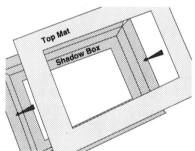

Cut the top mat and attach to the shadow box.

Select the mount board. Make it the same size as the top mat and attach objects.

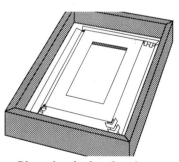

Place the shadow box in the frame.

Place the mount board behind the shadow box with the objects showing through the window. Close the frame.

Open Arcs

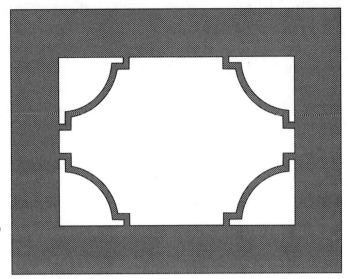

There are many steps involved in cutting this mat. <u>Don't</u> <u>read</u> <u>ahead</u>.
Follow these instructions, one step at a time, on a practice mat.

Materials: Alto's 4501 or 4505 Mat Cutting System, Alto's Model 360 Circle Cutter, an 11" x 14" piece of matboard, a very sharp pencil, and a soft eraser. As always, precision drawing with a sharp pencil and exact cutting with a sharp blade are necessary for a high-quality mat.

1 Set the 4501 or 4505 dimensioning system at 2" and draw four reference lines on the back of the matboard as shown (**Diagram A**). These lines will be the window opening reference lines.

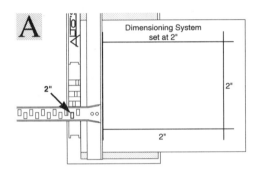

2 Set the dimensioning system at 2-1/4" by moving the arms up two posts. Draw two short intersecting lines in the corners of the window opening lines as shown (**Diagram B**). Repeat for all four corners.

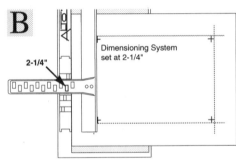

3 Set the dimensioning system at 5" and draw two 3/4" lines as indicated by "a" in Diagram C, just crossing the window opening reference lines from Step 1. Turn the mat one-quarter turn and repeat until all four sides are completed (eight lines total).

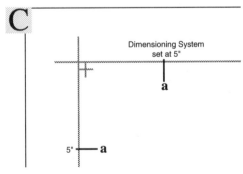

4 Set the dimensioning system at 2-1/2" and cross each of the eight lines you drew in Step 3 with a short 1" line as indicated by "b" in Diagram D. Again, this makes eight lines total.

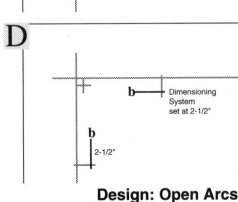

For a complex mat like this, success comes one step at a time.

Design: Open Arcs

5 Place a scrap piece of matboard over a piece of plywood to create a cutting surface for the Model 360 Circle Cutter. Place the mat on it. Remove the centering tack from the Model 360 and push it through the exact center of the + made in Step 2 (**Diagram E**). This is the "arc center" for the curved cuts you will be making. Make certain the tack punctures the matboard all the way through. Repeat for the remaining three corners.

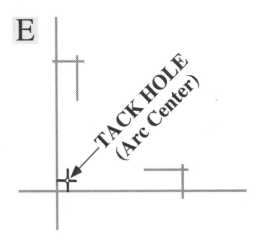

E

TACK HOLE
(Arc Center)

6 Place the centering tack in the arm of the Model 360 in the hole marked 4-3/4". Position the Model 360 so the tack goes into one of the "arc center" holes. Push the tack completely through the back of the mat, the scrap mat cutting surface, and into the plywood. Make sure it is secure before cutting.

7 Cut an arc from "b" to "b" (**Diagram F**). Sink the tip of the blade in at the start line and stop when the leading edge of the blade touches the stop line. Repeat for the remaining three corners, using the tack holes already made. Check the front of the mat after each cut to make sure you cut all the way through.

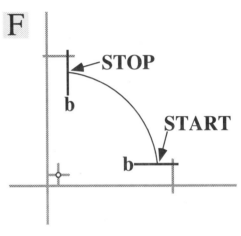

F

STOP

b

START

b

Detail F

STOP

b

8 Set the dimensioning system at 2-1/4". Turn the matboard over so the front (colored side) is up and place in the Mat Cutting System. With a pencil, *lightly* draw eight short lines, one at each end of each of the four arc cuts, just as shown (**Diagram G**).

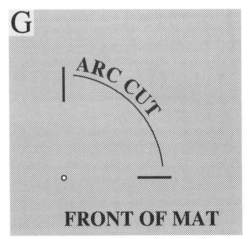

G

ARC CUT

FRONT OF MAT

9 Place the centering tack in the arm of the Model 360 in the hole marked 4-1/4". From the front of the matboard cut an arc from the start line to the stop line (**Diagram H**).

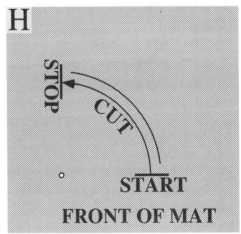

H

STOP

CUT

START

FRONT OF MAT

10 **Turn the mat over, face down.** Freehand draw curved lines as indicated by "c", precisely halfway between the ends of the two arc cut lines as shown **(Diagram I)**. Follow the curve of the arc cuts when drawing, and be sure to extend your freehand line "c" on both sides of line "b" as shown. Repeat on both ends of the arc in the remaining three corners of the mat, for a total of eight lines.

11 **Still on the backside of the mat, set the dimensioning system at 5", and slide the mat *under the straightedge and over the stops* as shown (Diagram J).**

The next sixteen cuts will be made with the mat in this general position, over the stops with the straightedge lined up by eye with previously drawn pencil lines along the far edge. These will be referred to as far cuts*. Each of the four edges of the mat will have two sets of two far cuts, one lined up with the lines "a", and one set lined up with lines "b".

12 **With the mat in the far cut position, line up the straightedge with two of the "b" lines (Diagram K).** When lining the straightedge up with the pencil lines, position the matboard as if you just drew those lines right next to the straightedge.

13 **For the 1st cut: Sink the blade 1/2" or so before the nearest arc cut and stop the cut on line "a"** (Diagram L).
For the 2nd cut: Sink the blade on the next line "a" and cut until 1/2" past the inside arc cut line **(Diagram L)**. Repeat for the remaining three sides.

*Far cuts are cuts made farther, or beyond, the standard reach[1] of the dimensioning system. For many of you this concept will not become clear until you actually do it. For this Open Arcs mat, there are <u>four</u> far cuts on each side of the matboard.

[1] The standard reach of the 4501 dimensioning system is 6". The 4505 dimension system will reach out to 8".

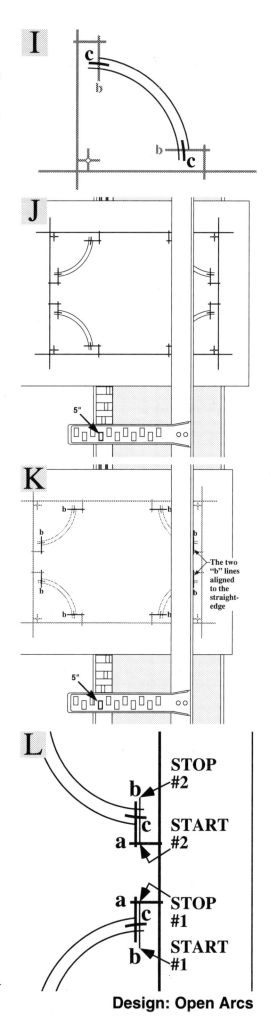

Design: Open Arcs

14 Slide the matboard out to the right 2-1/2" until the straightedge lines up with the two "a" lines (Diagram M).

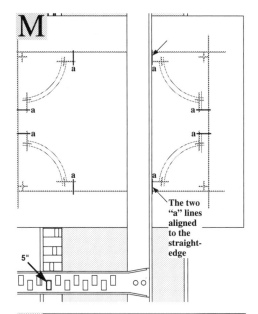

M

The two "a" lines aligned to the straightedge

5"

15 1st cut: Sink the blade tip into the window reference line closest to you, and cut until the blade's leading edge reaches line "b" as shown (Diagram N).
2nd cut: Sink the blade tip into the next line "b" and cut until the blade reaches the window reference line farthest from you (Diagram N).

16 Repeat Steps 12-15 for each of the remaining three edges of the mat.

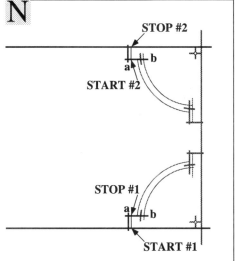

N

STOP #2
b
a
START #2

STOP #1
a b

START #1

17 Leaving the dimensioning system at 5", place the mat in the normal position (not the far cut position) with the back side of the matboard up.

18 Cut the two short lines as shown (Diagram O).
1st cut: Start the cut on the window reference line nearest you, stop the cut 1/4" past line "b".
2nd cut: Start the cut 1/4" before the next line "b" and stop the cut on the window reference line farthest from you.
Make these two separate cuts as directed—if you cut all the way across, the mat piece will fall out prematurely and make your last window cut difficult and sloppy. This is true for the next step as well. Now turn the mat a quarter of a turn and repeat until the remaining three edges of the mat are completed. You will have made eight cuts total.

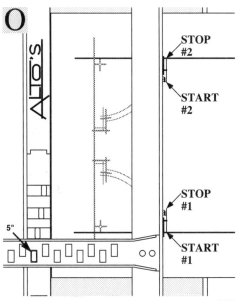

O

STOP #2
START #2

STOP #1

5"

START #1

19 Set the dimensioning system at 2-1/2" with the back side up. Make two cuts. **1st cut:** Start the cut with the blade tip sunk into line "c", the closest to you of the freehand lines drawn and lift the blade 1/4" or so past line "a" (**Diagram P**). **2nd cut:** Start cutting 1/4" or so before the next line "a" and end the cut on line "c" farthest from you (**Diagram P**). Turn the mat a quarter of a turn and repeat on the next edge until the remaining three edges of the mat are completed. You will have made eight cuts total.

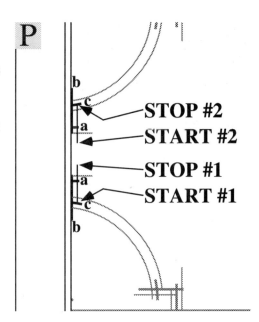

20 Set the dimensioning system at 2" and place the mat to cut the window opening. Each of the four sides of the window opening must be made in three cuts, not the usual one. If the window openings are cut in one continuous cut, the mat will not work.
1st cut: Start the cut on the window reference line nearest you; stop the cut when the silver mark on the blade holder (the cutting edge of blade) reaches the first line "a" (**Diagram Q**).
2nd cut: Raise the blade, move the cutter forward 1/4" and reinsert the blade tip precisely on the same line "a" which you stopped your last cut on. (Yes, you really are starting on the line you just stopped your last cut at.) Cut until the blade touches the next line "a" (**Diagram Q**). Lift the blade again and move the cutter forward 1/4".
3rd cut: Reinsert the blade tip precisely on the same line "a" at which you stopped the last cut, and stop the blade on the window reference line farthest from you (**Diagram Q**). **Repeat for the remaining three sides of the window opening**.

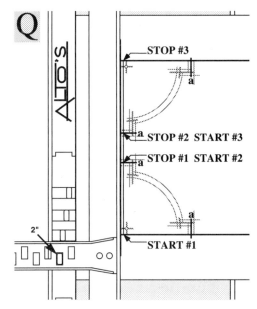

21 Gently erase any pencil lines from the front of the mat.

With a mat this delicate, if pieces don't fall out due to undercuts, DO NOT try to replace the mat in the dimensioning system to recut. Instead, simply use a sharp razor blade, inserted into the cut at the proper angle from the front of the mat. This is preferable to tearing corners out, or making overcuts. (See 4501/4505 instructions, "Finish Work" p. 8.)
This fancy mat can be used as the front mat for the shadow box mat. It is also lovely as a double mat, with the second mat a plain or fancy cornered undermat with the window opening dimensions 1/4" smaller than this one. Try the two mats in different color combinations.

Deco Corners

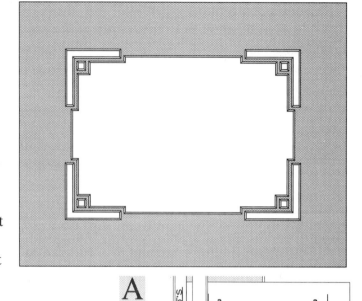

There are many steps involved in cutting this mat. Don't read ahead. Follow these instructions, one step at a time, on a practice mat.

Materials: Alto's 4501 or 4505 Mat Cutting System, an 11" x 14" piece of matboard, a sharp pencil. As always, precision drawing with a sharpened or fine-point mechanical pencil, and exact cutting with a sharp blade, with the correct depth adjustment, are necessary to succeed with this delicate mat. After each cut, check your cut to make sure it went all the way though the matboard.

1 **Set the dimensioning system of the 4501 or 4505 at 2" and place the mat in it, face down.** Draw two "a" lines on each of the four sides, making eight lines total as shown in **Diagram A**. The lines should intersect in each corner and be approximately 4" long. Labeling the lines may help when learning this mat.

2 **Move the dimensioning system to 4-1/2" and draw two "b" lines which intersect the lines from Step 1.** Draw them approximately 1" long. Repeat for the remaining three sides of the mat (**Diagram B**).

3 **Set the dimensioning system at 2-1/4" and draw four "c" lines (one each side), which connect the "b" lines from Step 2.** Do not cross the "b" lines with the "c" line, only connect them as shown (**Diagram C**).

4 **Set the dimensioning system at 2-1/2" and draw two "d" lines exactly as shown in Diagram D.** The lines should intersect the "b" lines and cross each other in each corner of the mat. Repeat for the remaining three sides of the mat.

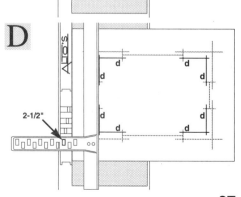

5 Set the dimensioning system at 3" and draw two short "e" lines to form a box in the corner of the intersection of the "d" lines from Step 4. The "e" lines should cross one another, but they should only touch the "d" lines, not cross them. See illustration (**Diagram E**).

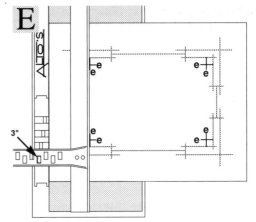

6 Set the dimensioning system at 5". With the backside still up, slide the mat under the straightedge so that it is on top of the stops as shown (**Diagram F**).

All the following cuts in Steps 7-13 will be made with the mat in this position (one end over the stops and the other under the straightedge). The straightedge will then be lined up by eye with the pencil lines previously drawn. These type of cuts are called far cuts*. Each edge of this mat has three sets of far cuts.

7 Line up the straightedge in a far cut position with the "d" lines drawn in Step 4 (**Diagram G**).

8 Make two short cuts as shown (**Diagram G**).
1st cut: Be sure to press down on the straightedge to keep the mat flat. Sink the blade tip at a point <u>halfway between</u> lines "a" and "d" closest to you, <u>not on the "a" line</u> closest to you (**Diagram G**). Cut until the silver mark of the blade holder is over the "b" line closest to you.
Lift the blade and move forward to the next line.
2nd cut: Sink the blade tip into the "b" line farthest from you as shown, and cut until the blade reaches a point halfway between the next "a" line and the "d" line, <u>not on the line</u> farthest from you. Check your cuts to be sure the blade is cutting all the way through the matboard.
Before cutting each set of two, you may mark a dot halfway between lines "a" and "d" to assist you in where to start and stop the cuts.

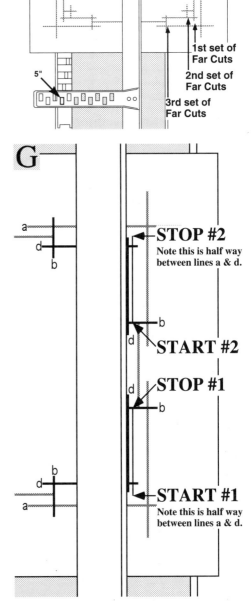

*Far cuts are cuts made farther, or beyond, the standard reach[1] of the dimensioning system. For many of you this concept will not become clear until you actually do it.

[1] The standard reach of the 4501 dimensioning system is 6". The 4505 dimension system will reach out to 8".

Design: Deco Corners

9 Slide the mat until the straightedge lines up precisely with the "e" lines drawn in Step 5. The mat should still be in a far cut position (**Diagram H**).

10 Make two short cuts as shown (**Diagram H**).
1st cut: Sink the blade on the "d" line closest to you and cut until the silver mark of the blade holder is over the "e" line. **Lift the blade and slide the cutter forward to the second "e" line.**
2nd cut: Sink the blade on the "e" line and cut until you reach the "d" line farthest from you.

11 Slide the mat until the straightedge lines up precisely with the "b" lines drawn in Step 2. The mat is still in the far cut position (**Diagram I**).

12 Make two short cuts as shown (**Diagram I**).
1st cut: Sink the blade tip on the "a" line closest to you, cut, and lift the blade when the silver mark of the blade holder is over the "d" line closest to you. **Lift the blade and slide the cutter forward to the next "d" line.**
2nd cut: Sink the blade tip on the "d" line and cut until you reach the "a" line farthest from you.

13 Rotate the mat 90° and repeat Steps 7-12. Then repeat Steps 7-12 on the remaining two sides of the mat.

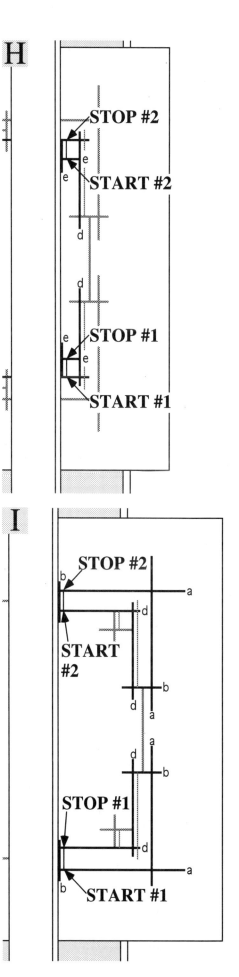

14 Set the dimensioning system at 4-1/2" and place the mat in face down. Make two short cuts as shown (Diagram J).

1st cut: Sink the blade tip on the "c" line closest to you and cut until the cutting edge of the blade cuts approximately 1/2" past the protruding end of the "d" line closest to you.

Lift the blade and slide the cutter forward to the second "d" line.

2nd cut: Sink the blade tip about 1/2" before the next "d" line and cut until the silver mark of the blade holder is over the next "c" line farthest from you.

Repeat exactly for the remaining three sides of the mat.

15 Set the dimensioning system at 3" and make two short cuts as shown (Diagram K).

1st cut: Sink the blade tip on the "d" line closest to you, and cut until 1/2" or so past the "e" line closest to you.

Lift the blade and move the cutter forward before the next "e" line.

2nd cut: Sink the blade tip 1/2" or so before the next "e" line and cut until the silver mark of the blade holder is over the "d" line farthest from you.

Repeat exactly for the remaining three sides of the mat.

16 Set the dimensioning system at 2-1/2" and make four short cuts as shown (Diagram L).

1st cut: Sink the blade tip on the "d" line closest to you and cut until the silver mark on the blade holder is precisely over the "e" line closest to you.

Lift the blade and slide the cutter forward 1/4".

2nd cut: Reinsert the blade tip precisely on the same "e" line you just stopped the last cut on and cut until 1/2" or so past the "b" line closest to you.

Lift the blade and move the cutter forward before the next "b" line.

3rd cut: Sink the blade tip 1/2" or so before the "b" line farthest from you and cut until the silver mark on the blade holder is over the next "e" line.

Lift the blade and slide the cutter forward 1/4".

4th cut: Reinsert the blade tip in the same "e" line you just stopped the last cut on and cut until the silver mark on the blade holder is over the "d" line farthest from you.

Repeat exactly for the remaining three sides of the mat. The little 1/4" squares should fall from each corner upon completion of this step.

If the 1/4" squares do not fall out, DO NOT try to replace the mat in the dimensioning system to recut. Instead, simply use a sharp razor blade, insert it into the cut at the proper angle from the front of the mat. This is preferable to tearing corners out, or making overcuts. (See 4501/4505 instructions, "Finish Work" p. 8.)

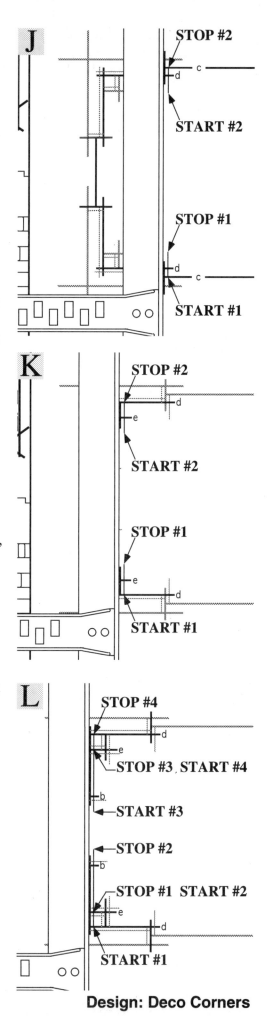

Design: Deco Corners

17 Set the dimensioning system at 2" and make two cuts as shown (Diagram M).

1st cut: Sink the blade tip in the "a" line closest to you and cut until the blade reaches the "b" line closest to you.

Lift the blade and move the cutter forward to the next "b" line.

2nd cut: Sink the blade in the next "b" line and cut to the "a" line farthest from you.

Repeat exactly for the remaining three sides of the mat. The L-shaped pieces should fall from each corner upon completion of this step.

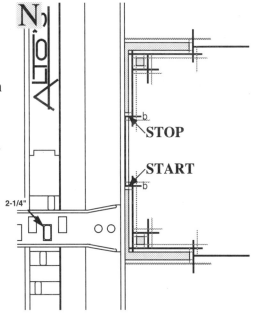

18 Set the dimensioning system at 2-1/4" and cut as shown (Diagram N), starting your cut precisely on one "b" line and cutting until the silver mark is precisely over the next "b" line. Repeat on the remaining three sides of the mat. The window piece should fall from each corner upon completion of this step, and your mat is complete.

With a mat this delicate, if pieces don't fall out due to undercuts, DO NOT try to replace the mat in the dimensioning system to recut. Instead, simply use a sharp razor blade inserted into the cut at the proper angle from the front of the mat. This is preferable to tearing corners out, or making overcuts. (See 4501/4505 instructions, "Finish Work" p. 8.)

This makes a marvelous top mat for a double mat. Simply use a complementary color of 11" x 14" matboard, and cut with window dimensions at 2-1/2" or more. For your second mat try using plain or fancy corner designs.

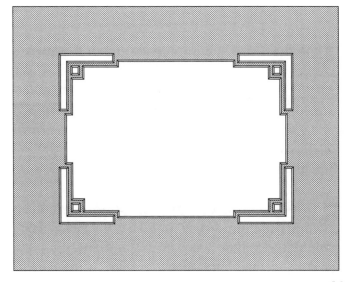

Southwest Thunderbird

*F*ollow the instructions and diagrams, one step at a time, on a practice mat of the correct size. **Read each step completely before you do that step. This pattern is more complex than some of our other designs. Do not be discouraged. If this is the first time you're cutting one of Alto's patterns, you may want to try one of our easier designs first. Plan to take at least an hour the first time you cut this mat.**

Materials: Alto's 4501 or 4505 Mat Cutting System, a **13" x 10-1/2"** piece of matboard, a sharp pencil, an eraser, a **30–60–90 triangle** whose hypotenuse (longest side) is about 14". As always, precision drawing with a sharpened or fine-point mechanical pencil, and exact cutting with a sharp blade are necessary for a high quality mat.

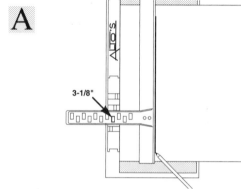

A

3-1/8"

1 Set the 4501 or 4505 dimensioning system at 3-1/8" with the matboard color side down. Draw one line across the long side of the mat (Diagram A).

2 Set the dimensioning system at 2-1/4" and draw the remaining three lines to form the mat's window opening reference lines. Erase all overlap lines as shown (Diagram B).

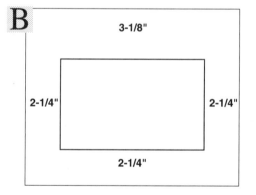

B

3-1/8"

2-1/4"   2-1/4"

2-1/4"

3 Set the dimensioning system at 2-7/8". Draw one line completely across the matboard on the 3-1/8" setting side. Label this line **"a"** (Diagram C).

4 Leaving the mat in the same position, set the dimensioning system at 2-5/8". Draw another line across the same side, labeling it **"b"** (Diagram C).

5 Leaving the mat in the same position, set the dimensioning system at 2-3/8". Draw another line on the same side, this time about 4" long and centered relative to the window opening lines. Label this line **"c"** (Diagram C).

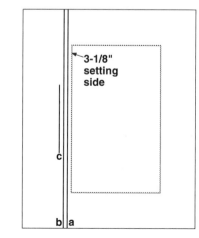

C

3-1/8" setting side

c

b a

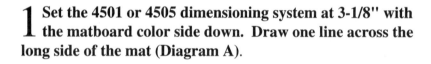

42

Design: Southwest Thunderbird

6 Turning the mat 90°, set the dimensioning system at 6". Draw a short line crossing line "a". Turn the mat 180° and repeat. Label these cross marks "d" (Diagram D).

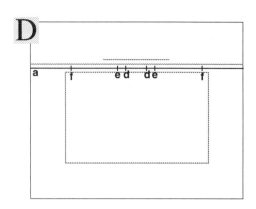

7 Leaving the mat in position, set the dimensioning system at 5-1/2" and repeat Step 6 on the new setting. Label these two cross marks "e" (Diagram D).

8 Repeat once more, but with the dimensioning system set at 2-5/8". Label these last two cross marks "f" (Diagram D).

9 Lay the movable cutting guide of the 4501 or 4505 aside. Place the matboard against the attached stops of the 4501 or 4505 so that the lines you just drew are at the top of the mat, and a short side is against the stops. **Place the triangle on top of the mat, with its shortest side against the stops and its hypotenuse at the top as shown (Diagram E).**

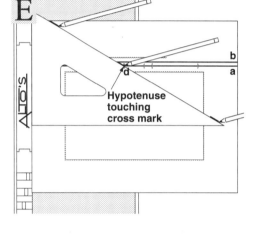

Hypotenuse touching cross mark

10 Slide the triangle up or down against the stops until **the hypotenuse** (the side of triangle opposite the 90° angle, and always the longest side of a right triangle) **touches the mark made by line "a" crossing the left most line "d". Draw a line against the triangle hypotenuse which connects lines "a" and "b".
Draw two 1/2" lines at either end of the triangle towards the edges of the mat (Diagram E).**

11 Draw tiny arrows pointing up to these lines AS SHOWN and mark them "g" (Diagram F).

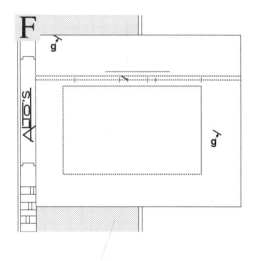

With this mat all of the arrows are *perpendicular (90°) to the lines, and pointing to the lines.*

12 Leaving the matboard in the same position, slide the triangle so that the hypotenuse touches the cross mark of line "a" with the left most line "e".
Draw a line against the triangle's hypotenuse <u>which connects lines "b" and "c"</u> – not "a" and "b" as with the previous line.
Draw two 1/2" lines at either end of the hypotenuse as **before**, this time drawing arrows pointing down to the lines.
Label them **"h"** (Diagram G).

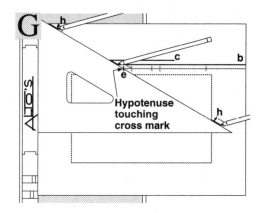

13 Leaving the matboard in the same position, flip the triangle over into the position shown (Diagram H), again with the short side against the stops. Slide the triangle up or down against the stops until the hypotenuse touches the cross mark made by line "a" and the left most line "f". Draw a short line as before against the triangle, this time connecting lines "a" and "b".
Draw two 1/2" lines at the ends of the triangle hypotenuse as **before**. Draw arrows pointing up to lines, and mark them **"i"**.

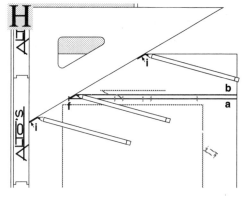

14 Turn the matboard 180° so the design you're drawing is at the bottom, and place the triangle (hypotenuse down, same as Step 13) over the mat, with both the mat and triangle against the stops (no illustration).

Repeat Steps 10-13 exactly, <u>except for arrow directions</u>. Draw the arrows in the <u>opposite direction</u> this time (pointing up to the lines if directions say down and vice versa). All arrows drawn are perpendicular to the lines. Label the lines with the same letters as before. The second time through Steps 10-13 do not refer to diagrams E, F, G & H since the mat and triangle will be in a flipped position from what the illustration shows. When you flip the triangle over the second time through Step 13, it will return to the original position of the hypotenuse up.

Design: Southwest Thunderbird

15 **Erase the extraneous marks around the design as shown, leaving 1" for line "a" and 3/4" for line "b" at the edges of the mat as shown. Do not erase the letters.** (Erasing the letters "d", "e", and "f" is ok.) Mark the two lines "a" and "b" with arrows pointing up (when the mat is positioned with the design at the bottom) with the arrow heads touching the lines as illustrated **(Diagram I).**

The left side of the mat is a mirror image of the right side. All of the arrows you have drawn should be the same as those illustrated here.

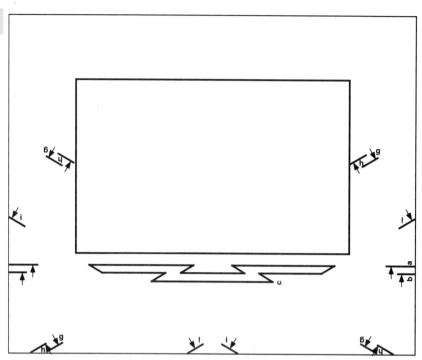

Cutting: For cutting the design part of this mat **you will be cutting on the pencil lines.** Line the cutting guide up with the sets of three short lines you've drawn in previous steps. Always make sure the arrows you drew are visible and pointing at the cutting guide. Hold the matboard firmly and move the cutting guide back 1/8" and cut on the pencil line.

16 **Return the cutting guide to a setting of 5-1/8".** Slide the corner of the mat over the stops and under the cutting guide with the design toward your right, <u>as shown</u>.

17 **Line up the three lines drawn in Step 10 marked "h" with the cutting guide as shown.** Be sure the arrows point to the cutting guide as described above **(Diagram J & Details 1-3).**

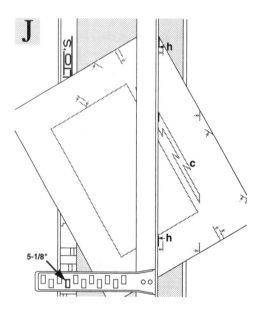

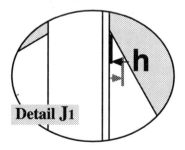

Detail J₁

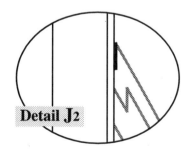

Detail J₂

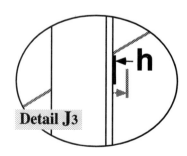

Detail J₃

Design: Southwest Thunderbird

18 Holding the mat down firmly so it does not move, change the dimensioning system to 5" and cut the short diagonal line connecting "b" and "c" (Diagram K). In order for the corner to come out, you must sink the blade **3/8" before** line **"b"** and cut until **3/8" past** line **"c"**. This overcutting will be necessary for all acute angle cuts on this mat (cuts where the angle made is less that 90°) **(Diagram K)**.

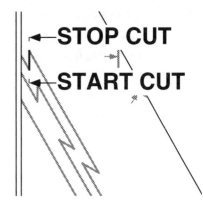

19 Set the dimensioning system back to 5-1/8" and rotate the mat *60° clockwise*. Insert the corner over the stops, under the cutting guide and line up the other line "h".

20 Holding the mat down firmly so it does not move, change the dimensioning system to 5" and cut the short diagonal line connecting "b" and "c" (Diagram L).

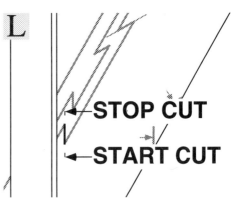

21 Set the dimensioning system back to 5-1/8" and rotate the mat *120° clockwise*, inserting the next corner in the same manner as before.

22 Line the straightedge up with the outer two lines marked "g" (arrows pointing toward the lines). Holding the mat down firmly, change the dimensioning system to 5" and **cut the short middle line as before,** starting and ending **3/8" before the beginning and after the end of line "g" (Diagram M)**.

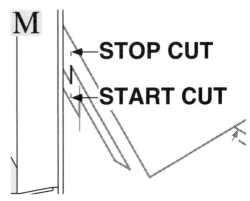

23 Set the dimensioning system back to 5-1/8" and slide the mat out to the right until the cutting guide lines up with the next set of three lines (the middle one will be the end of the design and the outer ones marked "i"). Hold the mat firmly and set the dimensioning system at 5" to cut the middle line. For this line, start your cut only **1/8" before** line **"b"** (this line is part of an obtuse angle—greater than 90°) and end **3/8" past** line **"a"** (this line is part of an acute angle, as explained in Step 18) **(Diagram N)**.

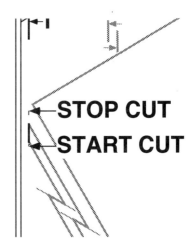

24 Set the dimensioning system back at 5-1/8" and rotate the mat *60° clockwise*, inserting the next corner over the stops and under the cutting guide as before. **Repeat Steps 22 and 23**. On the end of the design, cut as in Step 23, but this time it will be opposite, starting the cut at **3/8" before** the line and ending **1/8" after** the line since the acute angle is first this time.

Design: Southwest Thunderbird

25 Set the dimensioning system back at 5-1/8". **Insert the mat with the long design side over the stops and under the cutting guide as shown,** until the straightedge lines up with line **"b" (Diagram O)**. The arrowheads on line **"b"** will point to the cutting guide. You are going to <u>cut only the middle section</u> of the three parts of line **"b"**.

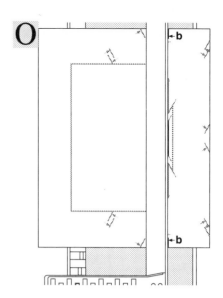

26 Hold the mat down firmly and set the dimensioning system to 5". Cut only the middle section of line "b". Start the cut **3/8" before** and end **3/8" past the line (Diagram P)**.

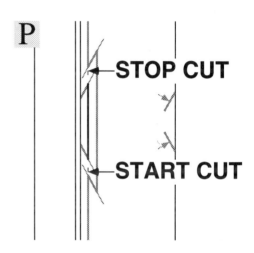

27 Set the dimensioning system at 5-1/8" and line the straightedge up with line "a".

28 Holding the mat firmly, move the dimensioning system to 5" and cut the two visible portions of line "a" as shown **(Diagram Q)**. Start the cuts **3/8" before** and cut until **3/8" past the line**.

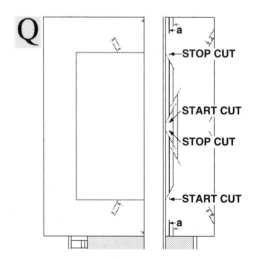

29 Set the dimensioning system at 2-1/2", rotate the mat 180°, and place in the system as you normally would, with the mat against the stops. The design is now on the left of the mat. Cut the two outside lines of line "b" (Diagram R), (you already cut the middle section in Step 26). Start the first cut **1/8" before** the line and cut **3/8" past**, but start the second cut **3/8" before** and cut **1/8" past the line** (the second line is opposite as it starts with an acute and ends with an obtuse angle).

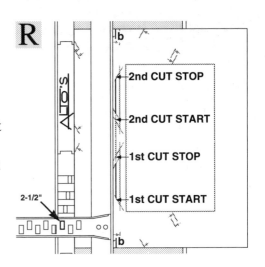

30 Leaving the mat in position, set the dimensioning system at 2-1/4" and cut line "c", starting 3/8" before the line and ending 3/8" past (Diagram S). The design piece should now fall out. If the piece doesn't fall out due to undercuts, don't pull it out or the corners will tear. Instead, insert a spare blade into the cut and gently finish the corner cuts. If you have undercuts or excessive overcuts, the next time adjust your start and stop positions accordingly.

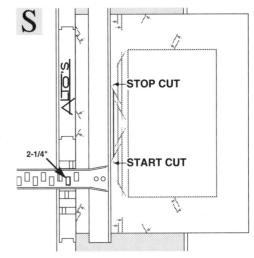

31 To cut the window opening, first set the dimensioning system at 3-1/8". Place the mat in normally to cut the design side of window (**no diagram**). **Return to using the lines as start/stop reference lines, instead of lines to cut on.**

32 Set the dimensioning system at 2-1/4" and cut the remaining three sides so the window falls out (Diagram T).

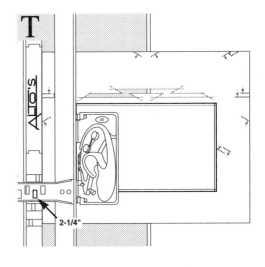

Congratulations! You've just finished one of the most difficult designs we have made. This can be made into a double mat by cutting another of a complementary color (see 4501/4505 instructions, "Double Matting – Method Two" p. 10), and adding 1/4" to the main window opening dimensions.

HELPFUL HINT
It takes practice to overlap the corners correctly on angle openings other than 90°.

This is the standard cut overlap for a 90° corner.

Obtuse angels (greater than 90°) don't need as much overlap to make the corners.

Acute angels (less than 90°) require a longer overlap.

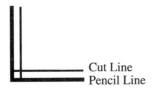

Cut Line
Pencil Line

Cut Line
Pencil Line

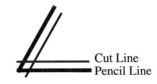

Cut Line
Pencil Line

Design: Southwest Thunderbird

Southwest Cardinal Points

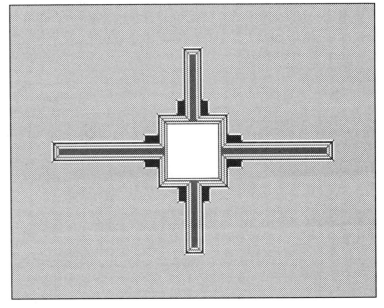

*T*his is a good design to take full advantage of the simplicity and speed of Alto's measuring system. This pattern is more complex than some of our other designs. If this is the first time you're cutting one of Alto's patterns, you may want to try one of our easier designs first. **Materials:** Alto's 4501 or 4505 Mat Cutting System, a sharp pencil, a good eraser, adhesive (such as double-stick tape), four pieces of practice matboard in complementary colors, sizes 11" x 14",

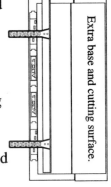

Extra base and cutting surface.

10-1/2" x 13-1/2", 10" x 13", and 9-1/2" x 12-1/2". If you have four pieces of matboard already pre-cut to 11" x 14", Step 1 is a quick and easy way to cut mats #2 , #3, and #4 down to the sizes needed for this project. Number your four pieces of matboard, with the top being #1, the next #2, etc. You will also need to extend your base because this project takes the dimensioning system to its limits and you will need to support the mat you will be cutting. Use a piece of 3/8" wood the approximate size of the base (if using the 4505, then 1/4" wood), with a scrap matboard for a cutting surface. This piece of wood will extend and be level with the base of your 4501 or 4505. If an extra piece of wood is unavailable, try seven or eight pieces of matboard, or some cardboard, to extend your base.

As always, precision drawing with a sharpened or fine-point mechanical pencil, and exact cutting with a sharp blade having the correct depth adjustment, are necessary to succeed with this complex mat. Check the blade depth after a couple of cuts to make sure the blade cuts all the way through the matboard.

1 **Do this step only if you are starting with four pieces of 11" x 14" matboard. Set aside mat #1 (top mat). Cut 1/2" off both the 11" and 14" sides of mat #2.** Set the dimensioning system at 2" and place the mat against the straightedge (not against the stops as you usually do). Hold the mat down, move the dimensioning system over one hole to 2-1/2" so the straightedge is on top of the mat. Cut the entire length of the mat. Repeat for the next side.

Cut 1" off both the 11" and 14" sides of mat #3, using the same technique by moving the dimensioning system over one additional hole to 3".

Cut 1-1/2" off both sides of mat #4 the same way, moving the dimensioning system to 3-1/2".

The proportional sizes of the four mats after cutting to size are shown here in **Diagram A**.

2 Place the additional base and cutting surface against the base of the 4501 or 4505. You will now draw and label the start/stop reference lines, and be drawing short reference edge lines for the top mat #1.

The sets of short lines drawn at the edges of the mat are for later reference when the second, third, and fourth mats are attached. **Labeling:** With this mat always use upper case letters, with the letter resting right next to the line as shown. Label the middle line, not the two short ones at the edges of the mat.

Dimensioning System Set At	Label	# of Lines Drawn	# of Edge Ref. Lines
1-3/4"	A	4	8
6-5/8"	B	2	4
5-1/8"	C	2	4
4-1/8"	D	2	4
5-5/8"	E	2	4
6-3/8"	F	4	
4-7/8"	G	4	
3-5/8"	H	2	
5-1/8"	I	2	

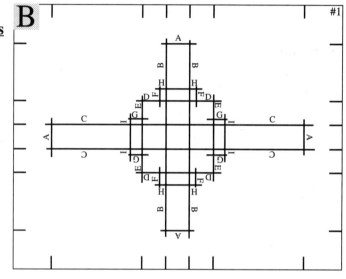

Draw all lines and labels exactly as illustrated (Diagram B).

Carefully erase the inside and excess lines as shown (Diagram C). On the reference lines for the inside corners leave about a 1/8" overlap, as shown. Make sure all the lines are clearly labeled on <u>both</u> ends, as the middle will be erased.

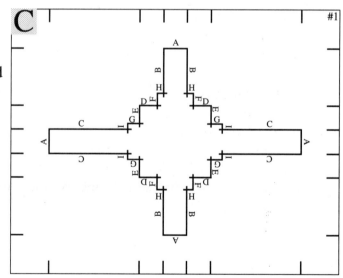

Design: Southwest Cardinal Points

Focus on EACH cut to see: – where is the START – where is the STOP – then, and only then, cut.

3 **You'll now cut this mat.** If you already understand the Alto's process, go ahead and cut this mat. If you are still uncertain, the chart below will take you step–by–step through the process. You will cut the short cuts first and then the long cuts. Each step, except lines B and C, will have two sets of lines labeled with the same letter: a first set—closest to you, and a second set—farthest from you.

For these cuts and for those that follow, make two cuts (instead of one all the way across). This will keep the window scrap in one piece for future use in these instructions.

Dimensioning System Set At	Cut From	To 1/4" Past	Cut From 1/4" Before	To	Rotate 180° and repeat
6-3/8"	H	D	D	H	Yes
5-5/8"	D	G	G	D	Yes
5-1/8"	G	C	C	G	Yes
4-7/8"	I	E	E	I	Yes
4-1/8"	E	F	F	E	Yes
3-5/8"	F	B	B	F	Yes
1-3/4"	B			B	Yes
1-3/4"	C			C	Yes
6-5/8"	A	H	H	A	Yes
5-1/8"	A	I	I	A	Yes

The window piece should now fall out. If it does not, finish the undercuts by inserting a sharp razor blade into the cut and finish the corners.

Replace the window piece in the finished mat, and apply sufficient adhesive to the back of the mat and window piece. Diagram D shows the pencil lines, cut lines, and double-stick tape on the back of the first mat and the second mat moving into position.

Permanently adhere mat #2, colored side down, to the back of mat #1, so that all four of its edges are inside the edges of mat #1.

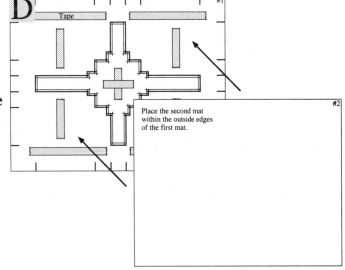

D

Tape   #1

Place the second mat within the outside edges of the first mat.   #2

4 You will be drawing and labeling start/stop reference lines for the next mat, #2.

Dimensioning System Set At	Label	# of Lines Drawn	# of Edge Ref. Lines
1-7/8"	A	4	8
6-3/4"	B	4	4
5-1/4"	C	4	4
4-1/4"	D	4	4
5-3/4"	E	4	4

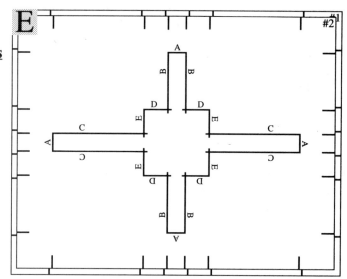

Carefully erase the inside and excess lines as shown (Diagram E). Make sure all lines are clearly labeled on <u>both</u> ends.

The reason for drawing reference lines on the outside edges of your mat is to provide an easy and quick cue that the start/stop lines on the second and third layer mats have been offset by the proper increments (in this case 1/8"). Outside reference lines marked on a particular mat should only be relative to the start/stop reference lines drawn for the following mat. Once you have attached a second or third layer, and you would like to check the setting of a start/stop line that is now hidden, the outside lines are a quick way to determine that setting. **Drawing outside reference lines is a good habit to get into when doing double, triple or even quadruple mats, regardless of its complexity.**

5 You'll now cut this mat. As in Step 3 if you are already familiar with the Alto's system go ahead and cut this mat. If not, the chart below will take you step-by-step. Each step, except lines B and C, will have two sets of lines labeled with the same letter: a first set — closest to you, and a second set — farthest from you. In cutting this and the next two mats, it is important not to undercut. Because these mats are connected to the previous ones, undercuts cannot be easily identified and finished with a razor blade.

Dimensioning System Set At	Cut From	To 1/4" Past	Cut From 1/4" Before	To	Rotate 180° and repeat
5-3/4"	D	C	C	D	Yes
4-1/4"	E	B	B	E	Yes
1-7/8"	B			B	Yes
1-7/8"	C			C	Yes
6-3/4"	A	D	D	A	Yes
5-1/4"	A	E	E	A	Yes

The window piece should now fall out.

Replace the window piece in the finished mat, and apply sufficient adhesive to the <u>back</u> of the mat and window piece. Diagram F shows the pencil lines, cut lines, and double-stick tape on the back of the second mat and the third mat moving into position.

Permanently adhere mat #3, colored side down, to the back of mat #2, so that all four of its edges are inside the edges of mat #2.

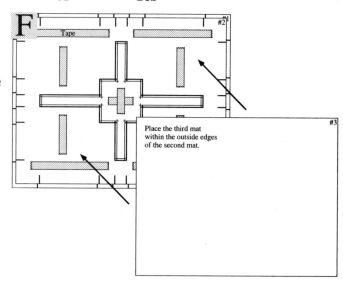

Place the third mat within the outside edges of the second mat.

52

Design: Southwest Cardinal Points

6 You will be drawing and labeling start/stop reference lines for the next mat, #3.

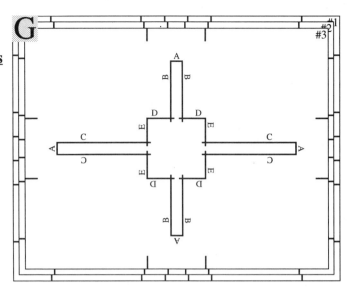

Dimensioning System Set At	Label	# of Lines Drawn	# of Edge Ref. Lines
2"	A	4	0
6-7/8"	B	4	0
5-3/8"	C	4	0
4-3/8"	D	4	4
5-7/8"	E	4	4

Carefully erase the inside and excess lines as shown (Diagram G). Make sure all lines are clearly labeled on <u>both</u> ends.

Please note that this mat has fewer outside reference lines. This is because the next mat of this project has only four related start/stop reference lines.

7 You'll now cut this mat.

Dimensioning System Set At	Cut From	To 1/4" Past	Cut From 1/4" Before	To	Rotate 180° and repeat
5-7/8"	D	C	C	D	Yes*
4-3/8"	E	B	B	E	Yes*
2"	B			B	Yes
2"	C			C	Yes
6-7/8"	A	D	D	A	Yes
5-3/8"	A	E	E	A	Yes

*Because the start and stop reference lines of these two cuts are so close to one another, be sure to pick up the blade after the first cut, move it forward, and reinsert for the second cut.

The triple mat window piece should now fall out.

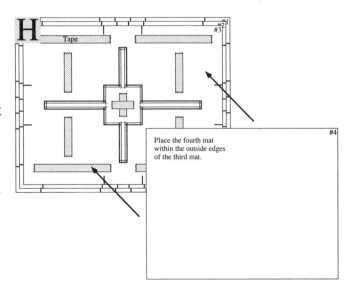

Place the fourth mat within the outside edges of the third mat.

Replace the triple mat window piece in the finished mat, and apply adhesive to the <u>back</u> of the mat and window piece. Diagram H shows the pencil lines, cut lines, and double-stick tape on the back of the third mat and the fourth mat moving into position.

Permanently adhere mat #4, colored side down, to the back of mat #3, so that all four of its edges are inside the edges of mat #3.

8 You will be drawing start/stop reference lines for the next mat, #4 (Diagram I).

The dimensioning system set at 4-1/2" and 6".

If you are cutting this mat with the 4501 Mat Cutting System the thickness of these four mats approaches the height of the dimensioning system posts. Hold the cutting guide firmly when cutting so the holes of the dimensioning system arms do not slip off the posts.

Cut all four sides.

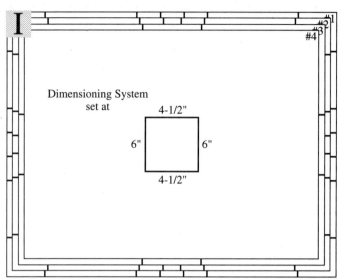

The quadruple thick window piece should now fall out. Turn the mat over. Looks great, doesn't it!

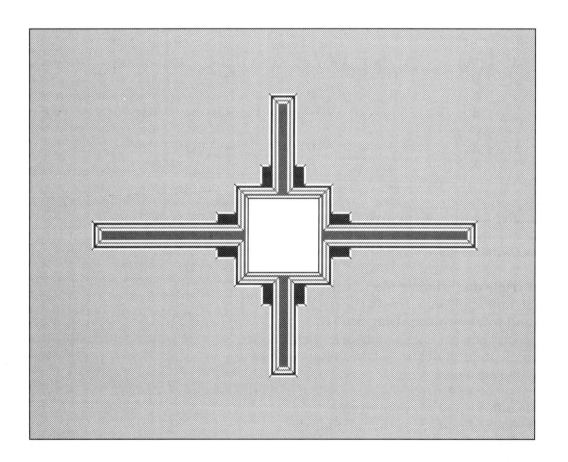

For larger mats, some of the cuts require the dimensioning system and mat to be set up like the drawing to the right.
(See 4501/4505 instructions, p. 14 for more assistance.)

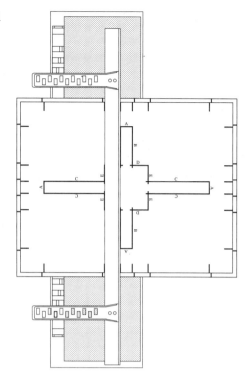

This mat looks wonderful if black core mat is used for one or more of the layers. If using black core matboard, you will need to change the blade with each mat. Black core dulls the blade edge quickly. As always, to ensure a clean sharp cut change the blade frequently. After you have practiced cutting this mat try some variations of this design.

A couple of the many variations possible.

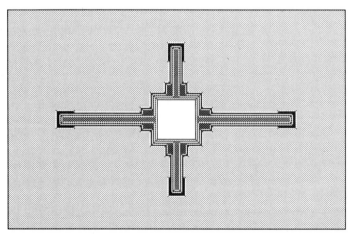

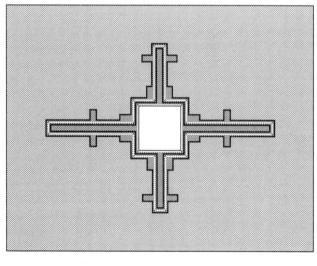

Design: Southwest Cardinal Points

Notes